Marriage! The Journey

From *Neediness* & *Myths* to God's Fulfillment

Promises:
p 156 - 158

ANNE TRIPPE

Marriage! The Journey

FROM NEEDINESS & MYTHS TO GOD'S FULFILLMENT

Essence PUBLISHING

Belleville, Ontario, Canada

Marriage! The Journey
Copyright © 2004, Anne C. Trippe

First printing November 2004
Second printing May 2005

All Scripture quotations, unless otherwise specified, are from the *New American Standard Bible*, copyright © The Lockman Foundation 1960, 1962, 1963, 1968, 1971, 1972, 1973. All rights reserved.

Scripture quotations marked KJV are taken from *The Holy Bible, King James Version.* Copyright © 1977, 1984, Thomas Nelson Inc., Publishers.

Scripture quotations marked NKJV are taken from the New King James Version. Copyright © 1979, 1980, 1982. Thomas Nelson Inc., Publishers.

All word definitions are taken from *Webster's New World Dictionary*, Copyright © 1957,. The World Publishing Company.

Library and Archives Canada Cataloguing in Publication

Trippe, Anne, 1940-

     Marriage! the journey : from neediness and myths to God's fulfillment / Anne Trippe.

Includes bibliographical references.

ISBN 1-55306-844-0.--ISBN 1-55306-846-7 (LSI)

  1. Marriage--Religious aspects--Baptists. 2. Marriage--Biblical teaching. I. Title.

BT706.T75 2004   248.8'44   C2004-905557-7

Essence Publishing is a Christian Book Publisher dedicated to furthering the work of Christ through the written word. For more information, contact:

20 Hanna Court, Belleville, Ontario, Canada K8P 5J2.
Phone: 1-800-238-6376 • Fax: (613) 962-3055.
E-mail: publishing@essencegroup.com
Internet: www.essencegroup.com

Printed in Canada
by

Essence
PUBLISHING

Dedicated to Vinson, my husband,
who has walked the Journey with me,
who loves me sacrificially and gives himself up for me;
and to our wonderful, supportive children
and grandchildren, who are gifts from God.
My Journey has led me into blessings
far beyond what I could have ever imagined.
For this I praise God and give Him all glory,
honor and praise forever.

Table of Contents

Foreword

Anne Trippe, who specializes in marriage and family counseling, is a member of our staff at First Baptist Church of Atlanta. Her book, *Marriage! The Journey,* is unique in that the focus is on learning to rely on the indwelling Christ to live out His life within marriage rather than relying on one's learned strategies, religious formulas and traditional marriage building principles found in many Christian books and seminars.

It is God's intention that fulfillment in marriage and maturity in Christ happen at the same time and in the same way. God's purpose is that Christ's passion, death and resurrection life be lived out in the marital relationship. This is the obedience required for all relationships in the body of Christ, but is specifically to be portrayed in marriage. It is by embracing God's grace and personal identity in Christ in relating with one's mate that fulfillment is found and inborn needs are satisfied.

Anne Trippe writes with clarity, helping us to identify a person's ineffective fleshly survival strategies. *Marriage! The Journey* confronts commonly-held myths about marriage and "roles," which is a provocative highlight. Explaining the Lord's purpose in adversity and how it relates to surrender to God in marriage is a main feature in the book. Understanding what responding to one's mate with the mind of Christ would look like is a turning point for couples. It is vitally important that the truths of life in Christ be presented in a clear, simple and engaging way to readers who likely have not been introduced to them. Anne achieves that in her book.

Dr. Charles Stanley
Senior Pastor
First Baptist Church of Atlanta

Introduction

Marriage! The Journey was written after many years of counseling hurting couples who found hope and fulfillment as they learned to walk in the truths explained in it. The book is a follow-up to the successful sixteen-week course, *Understanding Your Journey to Freedom in Marriage*. Many people came to me requesting the message be put in a book that could be available to everyone. Typical of the numerous comments to me are, "This is a message that desperately needs to be shared," and "The Body of Christ urgently needs this book."

My husband, Vinson and I have been best friends for many years, but we have encountered many of the same conflicts and discouraging times that other couples have experienced. Only as we learned of our union with Christ, His provision for us as individuals, faced some wrong beliefs we held about marriage and discovered how God intended to use the unfairness and hurts we experienced, did we come to know His freedom and intimacy in our relationship.

Marriage! The Journey illustrates aspects of various individuals' ventures into adulthood and marriage and their learning to take a higher road to personal power and satisfaction with each other. This is a spiritual journey designed and mapped out by God and symbolized in the account of the journey of the Children of Israel from Egypt to Canaan.

I have created composite characters whose pain, struggles, questions and discoveries are representative of couples I have counseled. I have chosen to describe, through a counseling setting, a little of their histories and their false beliefs about how needs are to be met within marriage. These partners are led into an awareness of their old survival strategies; then they discover how to walk in God's truth.

You will read of weary couples lost in defeating cycles of conflict in the desert—the wilderness area of their journey. After this, they find springs of water as they learn of God's grace and their union with Christ. I describe how they struggle to surrender old patterns and enter the promised land—their personal Canaan—and the Lord's fulfillment in their lives together. I answer their questions such as why God allows adversity and a spouse's sins and imperfections in marriage. I describe how to fight and respond to attacks of "road rage" with God's weapons. The marital partners discover that God's design for marriage is not only for happiness but to bring us to holiness and maturity in Christ.

The couples learn biblical truth about husband and wife "roles" and what forgiveness means for them as they live in the marital relationship. Finally, individuals recap their journey and personal discovery of the meaning of sacrificial love and what it looks like as they live with their mate.

Part One

DIFFICULTIES AND DISAPPOINTMENTS

Chapter 1

Hurt, Angry and Confused

"I admit it. I get extremely angry when she refuses to give me what I need. I just want some space and some peace from constant talk and demands. Sex is almost non-existent. Our conflicts are never resolved. We argue over the smallest issues and every discussion always progresses into a major blow-up. I am sick and tired and ready to leave." Darryl was hot.

Carol spilled hurt. "I know God didn't intend for my marriage to be this way. Aren't we supposed to agree? Shouldn't we enjoy doing things together? Why am I so lonely? What is marriage *for*, anyway?"

I hear other comments such as, "Rarely have my needs been met in my marriage. My husband/wife rejected me on our honeymoon and doesn't even touch me sexually. What is wrong with *me?*" Others ask, "What's the problem with *her/him?*"

George said, "When we were dating, I never had a clue it would be like this. She has changed so much. This hasn't happened to anyone else I know. What went wrong?"

Latoya was tense and drawn. She was confused when she said, "When I tell my family about our problems, they say it is my husband's fault and I shouldn't stay and endure the pain any longer. As a Christian, I don't believe in divorce, but I don't know if I'm willing to stay in the relationship if I can't be sure I can trust him."

Another person asked, "What kind of God would allow this kind of pain? It is not right and it is not fair."

A wife told me, "Everyone at church thinks my husband is so spiritual, but he's not like that at home. I am doing everything I can to get him to take responsibility and be involved with me and the family, but he only withdraws and gets angry—even verbally abusive." Her questions were urgent. "Why do I have to be the one who is responsible for keeping things from falling apart? It is all on me. I can't respect him. Isn't he supposed to be the head of the house and protect and guide us?"

I remember Tony's slow, gravelly voice. "It is so unfair that I give so much more than she does and I have nothing to show for it. She is so irresponsible. She never keeps house. If anything is ever done, I have to do it. She never considers my opinions. She never stops criticizing and it devalues me as a man. I deserve more."

"My husband always has to prove he is right and he gives solutions, but that is not what I need. I need him to listen and understand me and not be emotionally absent. He withdraws and is withholding. I need him to accept me and adore me," Mattie lamented.

Just recently, a man in ministry struggled to share a feeling often expressed by either husbands *or* wives, "There is no emotional intimacy between my wife and me. I am just left empty."

His wife countered, "If he loved me, he would intuitively know what I need and want. If I have to *ask* for something, it won't mean anything if I get it."

Katrina's assertions about her husband were caustic. "He had the audacity to bring me flowers, give me warm hug and 'thank me for a great performance in the bedroom' when he never shows he cares about *me* as a person. He never listens and never values me. It makes me want to throw up."

These remarks are typical of those I hear as a marriage counselor. Some express their pain loudly and forcefully while others fight silently and withdraw. Others "mind read" and play emotional guessing games, then try to "fix" their significant other. All attempt to control. Many try to calm the waters, please and manipulate in an effort to find validation from the spouse and avoid rejection. Whatever marital partners do, they are doing more of the same and, consequently, are *getting* more of the same as they relate in circular patterns and go nowhere.

To correct what is wrong, they go to marriage retreats and Christian seminars on how to have loving relationships. They learn communication skills, problem-solving techniques and religious principles to apply to marriage. Countless individuals read self-help books on how to draw boundaries and build their mate's self-esteem. Some pray hard, work hard, cry hard and, yet, feel as if they are dying inside.

How can this be? What has happened? We may have found that we are very different than our spouse. Why are we attracted to those who seem to block us, resist us, or demean us?

It is not just individuals and couples in counseling who experience hurts in marriage. Everyone, at some point, has suffered disappointment, felt shut out, known betrayal, or experienced the pain of not being valued by their mate.

There are seasons when every couple has emotions of hopelessness, anger, guilt, depression and fatigue; they wonder if they are willing to take anymore. Marital partners find themselves wounded and broken-hearted and God's peace seems distant. Their relationships are defined by failed attempts to find acceptance, completeness and fulfillment with their spouse. And they are left feeling *tired.*

Jeff Van Vonderan, in his book, *Families Where Grace is in Place,* created the acronym, T.I.R.E.D. "T"—*Trapped,* "I"— *Indicted,* "R"—*Responsible,* "E"— *Exposed,* "D"—*Defensive.* This describes the condition of numerous individuals in their marriages.

We are about to follow several couples on their journeys out of this wilderness and into God's best for them as they live in relationship with each other.

Struggling unsuccessfully to find acceptance, completeness and fulfillment in marriage leaves individuals feeling:

T   Trapped

I   Indicted

R   Responsible

E   Exposed

D   Defensive

Source: *Families Where Grace is in Place* by Jeff Van Vonderan, © 1992

Chapter 2

Beguiling *(Deceptive, Misleading)* Anticipations

Our car approached the white frame building sitting resolutely on an open hill. I became nostalgic. Years ago I sat alone on the front steps of the old country church and soaked in the summer meadow across the gravel road. Only the breeze whispering through the broomstraw, the cawing of a crow and the occasional buzz of a bee broke the silence. *Two eagles dipped and lifted high in the sun. My heart longed to ascend as if on eagles' wings and be filled with…something elusive that I couldn't identify.*

What was my yearning for? What was the neediness I felt? What was the key to satisfying that desire without a name? How could I find it? Perhaps it wasn't possible. Did others long for it?

I didn't know in my youth that a journey to fulfill that longing without a name begins for everyone the day they are born. I didn't know that people were searching and not finding. Society, books, the media and songs assured us our search would end if we found success and the right person—a soul mate, especially a soul mate.

The picture of the female singer on the black and white television that stood on the corner of our living room came in snowy, as they said back then. But she was beautiful, and the song was on the *Saturday Night Hit Parade*. It went something like this:

Will you fill my emptiness
and drive away my loneliness?
Will you promise you will be true to me
and always treat me tenderly?
Will you sigh with me when I am sad,
and will you smile with me when I am glad?

Think it over and be sure, and please don't
answer until you do.
And when you promise all these things to me,
*I'll give my heart to you.**

The song was full of what I refer to as *beguiling anticipations* or decep-tive, misleading expectations. She wanted to make certain that her hopes and dreams would be fulfilled by the right person. And she would only give herself in marriage to the one who would be attentive to her, support her, fill her and meet her needs. After all, that is the way love should be, shouldn't it?

This song was from another decade, but my husband and I have recently attended weddings where similar expectations were reinforced in the young couples. In one of the ceremonies, the officiating pastor had this exact exhortation for them. He stated that if things were the way they should be, this is the way they would be:

As the two of you truly join together as one,
each depending on the other,
you will feel no emptiness, no loneliness,
no cold nor pain.

This was a couple's hope for a new millennium! A time not so long ago that we thought would never come. A new age. And the expectations are not any different than those beguiling anticipations expressed in the song from years ago. The anticipations still exist and are more beguiling than ever.

---

* "If I Give My Heart to You," by Jimmie Crane, Al Jacobs and Jimmy Brewster [1953, 1954 (Renewed) EMI Miller Catalog Inc. All Rights reserved.] Used by Permission. WARNER BROS. PUBLICATIONS U.S. INC., Miami, FL.33014.

Times haven't changed our beguiling
anticipations for marriage:

A few years ago:

Will you fill my emptiness
and drive away my loneliness?
Will you promise you will be true to me
and always treat me tenderly?
Will you sigh with me when I am sad,
and will you smile with me when I am glad?

Think it over and be sure, and please don't
answer until you do.
And when you promise all these things to me,
I'll give my heart to you.

Today:

As the two of you truly join together as one,
each depending on the other,
you will feel no emptiness, no loneliness,
no cold nor pain.

We often think the years of Andy Griffith and the Cleavers were simple and more magical. But the restless yearning for one's neediness to be filled was the same then as it is today. And the anticipations were the same.

In the twenty-first century we perpetuate beguiling anticipations. The pastors at the recent weddings we attended, the world and, too often, the Christian community are offering expectations for marriage that elude our grasp. The words of the above song and of the marriage ceremony hold the unquestioned belief that if we select the right person, we can have a relationship in which our partner will fill us, support us, complete us—and we will find the joy, contentment, security and acceptance for which we have so longed. *And* we will live happily ever after.

The newly-weds were even promised freedom from experiencing pain, cold and loneliness if they would only depend on each other! So things haven't changed after all. These expectations have existed from the beginning and have birthed many myths about marriage and our closest relationships.

By the way, on the morning after one of those recent weddings, a preacher on the radio said men and women should get married to overcome loneliness, emptiness and various weaknesses. He said that when two become one, they are each complete in every way.

A pervasive view in Christian marriage seminars and self-help books is that if we marry opposite personalities, then our partners will complement us and complete us where we are incomplete, and we will do the same for them. In religious circles this idea is sometimes illustrated with a broken eggshell where the two broken parts are supposed to fit together perfectly to make a whole. This is touted as a correct picture of marriage. On the other hand, we are often encouraged to marry someone who is *similar* to us, someone with comparable likes, desires, interests, expectations and opinions. And when we do, we are surprised to find, after the wedding, that we are very different!

With whomever we marry, when things do not go well, we see our partners as having failed us. We feel T.I.R.E.D., betrayed and trapped and wonder what happened. Or we conclude that we made a grave mistake in marrying that person.

When our neediness isn't satisfied and our hopes aren't realized, we feel lonely, angry and hurt. We try to manipulate our partners to give us what we need, but that usually fails. Then we may turn to those who promise that the relationship would be right if we only practiced some good relational skills. So we do the seminar shuffle and pray that the Lord will change our mate to be that godly person he/she should be. We take lessons in reflective listening, sexual awareness, conflict resolution, encouraging our other and learning to respond to our partner's desires. All of this may include making hurtful lists about how our partner has failed us. And we pray.

We practice our new skills and we trust that our partner will then change and, in turn, give us what we need. However, that seldom happens. Either we fail to live out these new behaviors or they become a one-way street without any reciprocation by the one we love and we feel like martyrs. We continue in circular patterns of defeat while songs still promise fulfillment and happiness from our marital partners. One tells you that "I can't live without you." Another lets you know that "without you I am half, not whole." Yet another begs you to "please fill my hungry soul." The next one pleads for you to "set me free by loving me." These songs reflect real thinking that one's partner is to be the source of one's life, emotional well-being and completeness. Yet another says the way love ought to be is "subliminal, pivotal," and a "feeling of centrifugal motion"!

Yesterday the music lifted me. The singer told me I am the very breath he takes and every step he makes; easing his troubles is what I do. I take away his sadness and fill his heart with gladness as our two hearts beat as one. When I stopped the car and the music quit, the sublime vanished and I walked into reality.

I know today that inborn desire I couldn't name was a yearning for needs of fulfillment, acceptance and connectedness to be satisfied. When these needs aren't met and our great anticipations are not realized in marriage, we go to inconsiderate, unfair, disrespectful and disloyal extremes to get our companions to *give* us consideration, fairness, respect and loyalty. When we do not get it, we know how to inflict pain. We want them to hurt the way we've been hurt.

Is there a way out of this fighting and into God's best for us within marriage? Is it possible to experience the satisfaction we yearn for? The answer is, "Yes!" You are about to discover that there is even a road map to guide you on your journey out of this wilderness and into God's promised freedom and fulfillment as you live in your marital relationship.

Part Two

BEGINNING THE JOURNEY

Chapter 3

The Map and the Journey: Reading Directions

"We long to be free from old defeating patterns of relating. And we can. But first, we need to know where we are in order to know how to get to where we want to be, and God provides a map for us for this purpose," my friend Kay Ruff said.

I didn't even know God had a map, much less where I was on a map that reflects God's intention for us. In order to find God's solution to our marital dilemmas, we must consider the journey God has designed and mapped out for us.

Without getting too theological or complicated, The Map is a picture of the journey God's chosen people, the Israelites, took from Egypt through the Red Sea into the wilderness and then across Jordan into the promised land of Canaan. This was hundreds of years before Christ, but God intended that this journey would be symbolic of a Christian's passage in life. It is also an illustration of the marital journey. We began in Egypt and our destination is Canaan.

On The Map, Egypt depicts the time of the Israelites and ourselves living in captivity. It represents our being spiritually enslaved by the world system, sin and Satan. It is when we begin being programmed by our sin nature and influences such as family, culture, trauma and even religion. Egypt is where we began to learn what I will refer to as "survival strategies" for our journey through life and marriage. The Israelites leaving their slavery and crossing the Red Sea is like the believer's new birth or salvation experience when he is freed from having to live captive to the power of sin. But the new Christian moves baggage packed with old beliefs, hurts, traditions and survival strategies across the Red Sea and into a wilderness area of living, just as the Israelites did.

The Israelites became lost in the wilderness and wandered in circles for years because they were living out of their old ways—even mixing them with God's rules or laws, which led to failure and lack. They were not experiencing God's promises and their inheritance in the land of Canaan. It is the same with us. The wilderness is where Christian couples find themselves caught in power struggles and defeating patterns of relating as they live out of baggage containing their old strategies.

The survival strategies we develop consist of *false beliefs* about who we are and how our needs should be satisfied plus the *behaviors and emotions that result* from those beliefs. I will call the false beliefs "myths." Myths are our personal rules or laws for living in life and relationships. Myths can even include religious rules and laws. These learned patterns are familiar. They may look good and seem right, but they defeat us without our realizing it.

It is God's intention that couples leave this wilderness of emotional turmoil in marriage by crossing Jordan and moving into Canaan, just as it was His purpose for the Israelites. On The Map, crossing Jordan represents exercising faith in God's truth while surrendering reliance on our old survival strategies. The land of Canaan portrays God's promised peace, fulfillment and abundance for us. The Lord told the Israelites that *He* brought them out of Egyptian bondage so that *they* might go in and possess the land of their inheritance—Canaan. This possession came to those who were willing to risk stepping out in faith to cross the river. The account of the Israelite's journey can be found in Genesis 37–Joshua 5. In the same manner, couples will possess Christ's freedom and fulfillment in marriage when they learn truth and step out in faith to enter their Canaan.

As we follow various couples through their journeys and discoveries in counseling, you will have an opportunity to identify some of your own myths for living in relationships. You will see your own circular patterns of relating with your mate. You can discover why you married that certain person and how the Lord intends to use your spouse in your personal walk to peace and fulfillment within your marriage.

On the following page is a short explanation of The Map, which is a pictorial representation of the journey of the Children of Israel from Egypt to Canaan. You may refer to it as you progress through the book. It can help you understand where you are on your own journey.

The Map of the Journey

Egypt represents the world system where we were influenced by our sin nature, family, culture, trauma, religion and so on, and where we began to develop survival strategies for our journey.

The Red Sea is symbolic of a Christian's New Birth and his union with Christ.

The Wilderness is where we get lost and stuck on our way as we live from old survival strategies—our personal laws or myths—in our relationships.

The Jordan River is a place where we surrender reliance on old strategies of relating in marriage.

Canaan is unfamiliar territory where we learn to fight with new weapons and experience God's promises within marriage.

THE MAP: The Journey

EGYPT	WILDERNESS		CANAAN
Old Programming Developed	**Freed from sin's power**	**Death to fleshly Strategies**	Ongoing SURRENDER
	The New Birth	SURRENDER	**Abundant Life**
Survival training		Jordan River	**Our Inheritance**
Learning Fleshly Survival Strategies for Satisfying Needs			**************************
	Which way?		**FULFILLMENT**
	My Own Way		**************************
Influence from Families, Culture, Religion, Media, and the power of our Old Sin Nature	Freedom		**Needs satisfied**
	Being *LOST* in Wilderness		**Walking After the Spirit**
Red Sea	**Walking After Fleshly Survival Strategies & Law**		
Bringing our Baggage (Survival Strategies)			
Bound By Sin	Power Struggles	Leaving	Cleaving

Chapter 4

In the Beginning: Needs and Weeds

> **On the Map:** In Egypt where survival strategies are developed under the influences of sin, family, culture, trauma, religion and so on.

Some people say they knew they made a mistake as early as the honeymoon when their partner refused to have sex with them. One woman said she first saw her new husband change at the wedding reception when he shoved her, spilling punch on her dress. I see a growing number of couples who are disillusioned a few weeks after the wedding. Then there are those who recognized red flags before the vows were said and ignored them. One woman said that, standing at the back of the church waiting to walk down the aisle, she realized she was about to make the biggest mistake of her life.

We may believe our marital difficulties began when we married, when a child was born, when our spouse lost a job, when he or she first rejected us, or when some addiction became apparent. But the problems did not begin yesterday. It is unlikely that either partner woke up one morning and *suddenly discovered* that things weren't working. This awareness usually happens gradually where pretending, "pleasing," withdrawing, blaming and demanding build over time. The problems did not begin when they were first realized. They did not even begin with the wedding.

We bring into marriage conscious and unconscious beliefs about husband/wife "roles" and about how the relationship should work. Early in our growing-up years in the context of families, church, media, culture, school and peers, we draw conclusions about how emptiness should be filled, how loneliness should be driven away and how we can manage to live emotionally.

These impressions were formed during that time of our survival training. As we journey into adulthood, our beliefs are reinforced by many influences. Then, when we don't find what we anticipated as we relate to our marital partners, we are left bewildered. Conflicts come. But we must go back even further than families, culture or church to find where the problems really started. We must go to a place "long ago and far away," as they say in story books. We must go to the beginning to uncover how humanity's deep desire for needs to be satisfied all began. Of course, neediness originated in a garden.

I like gardens. Once upon a time when I was a child, my dad borrowed a mule every spring to plow up the ground so he could begin planting seed. On one occasion he let me help him hold the wooden plow handles, worn smooth from years of use, and call "gee" and "haw" to that mule so the mule would obediently pull slightly to the left or to the right to make neat, straight rows. I can still recall the aroma of that cool, dark, freshly-turned earth. I like manicured vegetable and flower gardens with neat rows of contrasting color and lawns with defined edges and no weeds. I imagine when Adam cultivated and dressed the Garden of Eden, it wasn't manicured with bordered and orderly rows, and that, in the beginning, there were neither weeds for him to pull nor any thorns that choked the plants.

When God created Adam and Eve and placed them in a garden to live and enjoy life, they depended on Him to satisfy all their needs and longings. They had intimacy with God and each other. They had no worries, conflicts or guilt. Everything was perfect for them. God had breathed the breath of His life into them and, as a result, they were satisfied and complete. All they needed was contained within His life. The couple didn't question their value. They were given peace and security from God.

God gave them a command to be fruitful and multiply. He also gave them one "do not" rule to obey as they lived in this garden. But something tragic happened. Adam and Eve disobeyed God and broke the rule. God pronounced a curse because of what they had done. They were separated from God and His life. Scripture calls this separation "death." They did not die physically but spiritually. Emotionally they were left empty and frightened. Since they no longer were connected with God's life, they were filled with shame and guilt. They were no longer complete. Adam and Eve no longer knew security, acceptance or contentment. Their thoughts and behaviors were empowered by sin because there was nothing good left in them. In fact, *sin* became who they *were*—their basic nature. *Neediness began* because of Adam and Eve's disobedience and God's curse.

Because of their disobedience, Adam and Eve had to leave the Garden of Eden. God's curse was on the ground as well. As a result, weeds and thorns came up and choked other growing things. Cultivating the ground and keeping plants, which had once been a pleasant duty, now became sweaty, tiring work and it was labor to even grow and find food.

Since it was so fatiguing just to keep up with the work and because Adam and Eve were emotionally and spiritually empty, tempers flared. *There was no option but to try to get by their performance and from each other what they had previously received so freely and unconditionally from God's life.* Neither Adam nor Eve had any peace or satisfaction. After the curse and after they were separated from the life of God, they lived independently of Him. It was in their nature to manipulate, control, blame, shame, withdraw and deceive in their relationship with each other to try to get what they so desperately needed.

But nothing they could devise worked to fill their longing to be restored to that former state of satisfaction and completeness. Before long they forgot it was God who had met their emotional and spiritual needs and they truly began to believe their emptiness needed to be filled by either their own or the other's performance.

Pride, which was in them now, made them think they could devise strategies, "shoulds," and "oughts" to gain what they had lost. It also caused both to believe they were entitled to get everything they needed and wanted from each other. They learned to make their manipulations look good so they could subtly trick each other into complying with their demands.

As Eve pulled weeds from her kitchen garden and struggled with managing the kids, she probably complained and yelled that Adam wasn't doing his share to help. Out of the sting of rejection, Adam must have angrily replied that she didn't appreciate him and his dawn-to-dusk efforts to find food and skins to feed and clothe the family. The Bible states clearly how God's curse would affect the husband/wife relationship. When we see this, we can grasp the reason for Adam and Eve's efforts at control and domination. *And when we understand that we inherited this state of being from our ancestors, Adam and Eve, we can begin to comprehend where our marital struggles began.*

As God pronounced the curse, He told Eve in Genesis 3:16, "Your desire shall be for your husband, and he will rule over you" (NKJV). The term *desire for* is the same one used in Genesis 4:7 when God warned Cain about the results of his rebellion. God said to Cain, "If you do well, will not your countenance be lifted up? And if you do not well, sin lies at the door; and its *desire is for* you, but you must master it" (emphasis mine). Here, "desire for" means that sin crouches at the door *waiting to control you or master you.* So in Genesis 3:16 when the same term is used, it means that living under the effects of sin and the curse, the wife will try to control the husband and he will try to rule over or control her! Remember, *this is the curse and not God's plan for marriage.*

The Lord's plan is that Christ provided the way so we Christians would be restored to that original state of completeness, having all needs being met by God, just as Adam and Eve experienced before they sinned.

Knowing that after Adam and Eve disobeyed God each of us inherited from them a sinful power that compels us to control, manipulate, hide, lie, fear and live out of guilt, shame and rejection, we can understand the root of our struggles. When we were born, we immediately began to attempt to fulfill our neediness by these methods.

God told Eve (Genesis 3:16) how the curse would effect the husband/wife relationship.

Remember, *this is effects of the curse, not God's plan for marriage!*

"Your desire shall be for your husband, and he will rule over you." The term *desire for* in Genesis 3: 16 is the same one used in Genesis 4: 7 when God warned Cain about the results of his rebellion. God said to Cain, "If you do well, will not your countenance be lifted up? And if you do not well, sin lies at the door; and its *desire is for* you, but you must master it." Here, *desire for* means that sin crouches at the door *waiting to control you or master you.* So we can see that in Genesis 3:16 when the *same term* is used, it means that living under the effects of sin and the curse, the wife will try to control the husband and he will try to rule over or control her.

Vinson and I have thirteen precious grandchildren. They are sweet, smart and affectionate. They are a heritage and blessing from God. As grandparents, we have been able to see how all are born with unique ways of approaching life to satisfy inherited needs. All have certain strategies for self-protection and for finding worth and acceptance. Nobody had to teach any one of them to blame or lie to justify themselves, to use self-pity to get attention, to hide for protection, to avoid pain, to be covetous, to control for things to go his way, to lie and to even "please" for validation. They all know instinctively. These attempts often even look quite good! It is in our very nature and identity when we are born to live under this power of sin and the curse. We have that natural "drive" to try to get our emotional longings met, protect ourselves and absolve ourselves of guilt. We learn in Ephesians 2: 1; 1 Corinthians 15: 22; Romans 5: 12 and Romans 3: 23 that this kind of separation from God and these effects of the curse were passed on to each of us from Adam and Eve.

The question of where our defeating cycles of relating in marriage originated has already begun to be answered. It began with what we inherited. What an *awful* inheritance! But there is more. To all this baggage we bring from birth, we must add our *perceptions* of the *type of family* in which we grew up. When we pile on the influence of our *culture*, any *trauma*, our *peers* and *religion*, or lack of it, we begin to discover where our concepts about ourselves and about how to satisfy our neediness came from. These early influences helped define our false beliefs and the resulting behaviors. Our beliefs and behaviors—*our own strategies*—are the *weeds* in our lives that choke out God's truth and keep it from being profitable to us.

In the next chapter, I will give examples of how false beliefs or *myths* are devised. However, it is not as important to know where they came from as it is to know what they are. You will have an opportunity to begin to discover some of your own myths about how your neediness is to be satisfied.

Chapter 5

Survival Training: Packing for the Trip

On the Map: In Egypt and perhaps in the wilderness. This is where we devise strategies for making life work. We begin developing these solutions in childhood, in Egypt, before our new birth.

"Fatty, fatty, two by four, can't get through the kitchen door," Rodney's third-grade voice taunted as we waited in line to board the yellow bus after school. (Well, *really*. I wasn't a blimp!) No harm was intended when Greg got the job of helping me with my survival training in the fourth grade or when Meg and others took over in the fifth grade, choosing me last for games at recess. Whenever and wherever I felt threatened, I learned to cover the nauseating tightening in my stomach and throat with a laugh or funny remark to anesthetize—or hide—the pain.

Years later, after my bulletproof vest and other protective gear, including my myths, were securely in place, I learned that I had gained weight as the result of a serious illness that kept me out of school for three months in the spring of the second grade. But my child's heart hadn't known that. I had gradually acquired some equipment for my journey— including invisible "receivers" sensitive to any possible enemy attack. Among the unconscious myths I developed were "I must stay guarded and not reveal anything about myself to stay safe" and "I am not acceptable."

Close to my tenth birthday I sat on the upholstered bench in front of Mama's Victorian vanity as she combed my hair and put a large blue ribbon in it to match my blue-dotted Swiss dress. I admired myself and I asked her if I looked pretty. Her stern reply that I had heard many times was, "Pretty is as pretty does!"

I instantly remembered an incident the day before when I had helped her put away some pot lids in the kitchen cabinet, evidently in the wrong place. Her familiar rebuke had been, "Why can't you ever do anything right? You grieve us so! You are a reflection on us. What will people think of us if you don't do things right?" I was accumulating more equipment for the trip as my survival training continued. As I traveled through my growing-up years, my protective armor was reinforced with more unconscious myths such as "I must be defective and a source of grief," "Worth is measured by good performance" and "I can never do enough to be acceptable."

When we are children, during that time of survival training for life's journey, we generate false beliefs about ourselves and about how to make life work to meet our inborn needs of **Contentment, Security and Worth.** **Contentment** means *peace, satisfaction, fulfillment* and *completeness.* **Security** means *acceptance, love, protection, stability* and *safety.* **Worth** means *value, significance* and *importance.*

I named the false beliefs "myths" because they are formed under that inherited drive of sin and involve self-effort, control and manipulation. **Myths always result in damaging emotions and defeating behaviors.** Remember that the *combined* myths and behaviors are what I refer to as our survival strategies.

Survival strategies and the protection, the acceptance and the *life* we hope they will bring are based on *performance or personality.* We even base our *identity* on these things. We devise ways to preserve ourselves, improve ourselves, avoid rejection, find acceptance and fulfillment in life and marriage. However, survival strategies are always self-defeating and never bring the satisfaction they promise. But they are all we have and when they don't work, we wonder what went wrong.

Scripture labels these strategies *flesh* and also uses the term *one's own way.* The word *flesh* in the Greek can mean "trying to make life work the best way I know how, in my own human strength."* Survival strategies can be either positive or negative. They can look good and seem reasonable. They can even be religious. Or they can be unacceptable and immoral. They can be people-pleasing and co-dependent, or guarded and passive, or perfectionistic and self-disciplined, or dominant and logical. They always include skillful defenses and coping mechanisms.

We have a tendency to think of immorality or "smokin', drinkin' and runnin' around" as sin. However, walking after *our own way*, after our own strategies, is how our independence from God and *self-reliance* is expressed. And this is sin, regardless of how it looks externally.

These false ways of thinking with the resulting behaviors may be unconscious to us, but when we walk in them, sadness lurks beneath the surface and discontentment, worries, doubts and fears are not far away. We believe our circumstances are to blame for our emptiness and anxiety, because we don't know that these problems are rooted in our trying to live independently from God and in our myths—in that wrong thinking we developed during the years of our survival training!

The strategies in the baggage that we bring into our adult relationships can look good and be well-intentioned, but they prevent us from experiencing the good things the Lord has provided for us. Some have correctly said our childhood strategies become adult problems.

Soon you will be able to identify your own ineffective strategies for living in life and marriage that are packed in your baggage.

---

* As Bultman expresses it, the word *flesh* represents "trust in oneself as being able to procure life…through one's own strength and accomplishment…Both legalism and lawlessness are (also) 'fleshly' in so far as they both hold out a false promise of life on the basis of man's efforts." (From *New International Dictionary of New Testament Theology*, Vol. 1, pp. 680, 681.)

Following is a summary of some of the points I have made:

WE ARE BORN NEEDY

Needs include:

■ **Contentment:** Peace, satisfaction, fulfillment, completeness.
■ **Security:** Acceptance, love, protection, safety, stability
■ **Worth:** Value, significance, importance.

Neediness

+

SURVIVAL TRAINING

Under the influence of:

▲ **Sin nature**
and our perceptions of:

▲ **Family**   ▲ **Religion**
▲ **Culture**   ▲ **Media**

Results in

SURVIVAL STRATEGIES

(Our myths and the resulting defeating behaviors
and damaging emotions)

Discovering Survival Strategies

When people come to me for counseling, I get a personal history to help me discern some of the strategies they constructed for meeting basic needs of **Contentment, Security** and **Worth**. I identify these myths and behaviors so they can "own" them and later contrast and replace them with God's truth. To illustrate how strategies can be formed, I will introduce you to some individuals and couples who are composites of those whom I have counseled. We will eventually follow them on their journeys out of the wilderness and into God's fulfillment in their relationships.

Mattie

Mattie was petite and conservatively dressed. Her chin-length, sun-streaked hair was hooked behind one ear. With her knees together and ankles crossed, she sat quite properly on one end of the sofa in my office. Her quirky right shoulder would tense and move forward if she felt threatened. The mother of two grade-school children was an English teacher who chose her words carefully and precisely. I later came to see Mattie as a steel magnolia, pious, social and intelligent. Mattie was also discouraged and depressed.

After she revealed something of the difficulty that had prompted her to come to counseling, I sent home a personal history questionnaire to help me discover some of the strategies she had devised for living life. Over the next couple of weeks, I learned that Mattie was born to parents who had loud disagreements but taught her that survival meant perseverance and having a good work ethic.

She learned as a child that she could feel safer and more acceptable by "pleasing" a demanding mother. As a result of her good performance and compliant ways, Mattie's parents built up her self-esteem through praise, yet they were very demeaning on the few occasions when she didn't measure up to their expectations. Mattie was self-confident, bright and an involved leader in school. Her activities brought many accolades. Later, as she worked to help with college expenses, Mattie's belief that being super-responsible paid off with personal security was reinforced. Years of being applauded and finding acceptance for her personality and performance became her survival training for the road ahead.

Without realizing it, Mattie's survival strategies involved relying on others' opinions of her as she carefully managed her behavior to avoid rejection. Lack of validation from a loved one meant to her that she didn't measure up. So in her dating and courtship, she had pursued relationships in which her responsibility and people-pleasing minimized conflict and brought the acceptance she had come to depend on. She was smart and rarely wrong, even about financial matters.

Mattie was on her journey. Upon inspection, her baggage was neatly packed with carefully selected equipment for whatever circumstance she might encounter. Among the strategies in her bags and trunks were myths such as (notice that *needs* are in bold):

- "I must be in control and be responsible to **be secure** and find **acceptance**"
- "I must do it right (or perfectly) to **be loved and appreciated**"
- "I must 'fix', remind, rescue and calm the waters to find **approval and be secure**"
- "I am entitled to praise from a significant other making me **feel valued**"
- "A job well done should bring **worth and acceptance**"
- "I need a person to be emotionally **secure**"
- "I must please others to avoid rejection, find **acceptance** and know I am of **worth**

We will re-visit Mattie as she progresses on her journey.

Darryl

Darryl had an average build. His salt-and-pepper hair was trimmed short and his clothes crisply pressed. His crossed arms and strong, guarded demeanor belied sensitivity, anger and hurt. I was to discover that he had rigid expectations of others and was intolerant of their mistakes. He was erudite and always had to be right. Darryl was matter-of-fact as he told me of his struggle to make it financially as a sales rep for a software company.

Everyone must go through his own survival training, and Darryl's bags and trunks were packed with some different items as he set out on the road of life. Darryl's training for his journey began in an upscale urban neighborhood. His father had been highly successful, a rigid perfectionist, emotionally distant and critical of mistakes in others. His mother was a people-pleaser, a caretaker and a "rescuer." She had a "victim" mind-set and knew how to place guilt trips on others to get them to placate her.

Both parents catered to Darryl and did things for him that he could have done for himself. As a result, he subconsciously decided that he must not be capable of taking on responsibilities. His father bailed him out of several disasters but criticized him severely.

Darryl learned that it was easier to withdraw and avoid responsibility than risk being criticized for not doing something right. He had developed the belief that being catered to meant that he was loved and secure. His friends saw him as a creative man who could talk a good Christian talk but sometimes displayed rage when they didn't give in to him.

His strategies contained myths such as:

- "I must avoid failure to keep my little sense of **worth**"
- "My being "catered to" means I am **loved and accepted**"
- "I must avoid being controlled in order to be my own person
- "I am entitled to my protective space"
- "I must perform perfectly to be **loved and accepted**," yet,
- "There is no way I can measure up!" but,
- "I am right and I must be heard to prove my **worth**"
- "Things must go my way for me to feel in control, **secure** and to find **approval**"

Darryl's trunks and bags bulged with several varieties of controls and escape mechanisms as his journey was under way.

These are some rather simple illustrations of how a person's myths and behaviors are constructed. *Each person works out his "own way" of attempting to control life and circumstances to find **Contentment, Security** and **Worth.***

Mattie's and Darryl's cases are not unique and neither was my own. These, and other strategies individuals develop for living in relationships, are typical. You will soon learn more of Darryl and Mattie and their life *together* as husband and wife.

We build a super-structure of controls and manipulations to find safety and acceptance. Our strategies may look good and work for a while, but sooner or later we find ourselves bruised and frustrated. When we are blocked from living out of our controls and "entitlements," which we believe should make life work for us, we become angry and T.I.R.E.D! Remember Van Vonderan's acronym. Regardless, our baggage for life's journey is well packed with many fleshly strategies by the time we reach adulthood and marriage.

Following is a page that can help you begin to identify some of your own myths and behaviors for satisfying your basic needs of **Contentment, Security** and **Worth.** Do not answer the questions "the way it should be in Christ," but define how you have attempted to meet these needs outside of reliance on Christ.

To begin identifying some of the beliefs you developed about how your needs should be met, complete this exercise.

MYTHS ABOUT HOW MY NEEDS SHOULD BE MET:

As you complete this exercise, **do *not* answer according to "the way it should be in Christ."** Answer how you have naturally wanted things to happen. You could have several answers for each.

Husband, kids, financial security _____ will make me **content.***

* Where have you looked and/or what have you done in an attempt to find contentment?

Need #1 — CONTENTMENT

(Contentment means: satisfaction, peace, fulfillment, being forgiven and so on)

Money, material goods _____ will make me feel **secure.***

* Where have you looked and/or how have you tried to provide a sense of security for yourself?

Need #2 — SECURITY

(Security means: safety, protection, stability, connectedness, acceptance)

Money, material goods _____ will make me feel of **worth.***

* Where have you looked and/or how have you tried to make yourself feel of worth?

Need #3 — WORTH

(Worth means: value, significance, importance, acceptance)

On the Road: Baggage inspection

I have described how some of the equipment for our journey can be acquired. Bags, trunks and chests are well packed and loaded with bullet-proof vests, well-constructed myths and boots made for walking. It can be helpful at this point to inspect your own baggage to discover some typical rules and myths you have brought on your journey.

It is valuable to know what our myths are, because they are the culprits behind our damaging emotions and ineffective behaviors. Myths are the fuel we rely on for our vehicles as we travel. Sadly, we will see that this fuel is defective and the cause of failure and emotional damage in marriage and along a road well traveled.

The goal of this book is that you move beyond your myths, struggles and disappointments to God's victory and fulfillment in your marital relationship. After identifying your myths or faulty beliefs, which I sometimes refer to as "the lies we believe," you will be able to replace them with truths from God's Word. As you proceed with our couples on their journeys out of the wilderness they are in, you will learn how to walk in these truths in your own marriage.

Scripture says that we are to *be transformed,* **not by the renewing of our behaviors, but by the renewing of our** *minds— our beliefs, our attitudes, our thinking* **(Romans 12:2). The word** *repentance* **even means turning around and going in a different direction by a** *change of mind!*

When we walk by truth rather than old myths, changes in our behavior and emotions will follow. Next, is a list of typical rules or myths by which we live. The needs are identified in bold type. Try to discern the beliefs that apply to you and highlight them. Add any that may apply.

MYTHS about Meeting Needs

Rules or "laws" for satisfying needs. **Needs** are in bold.
Notice that myths are *performance-based*. Some false self-concepts
are also listed. Check any statements that apply to you.

✓1. I must please others to avoid rejection and find **love and acceptance**.

2. I must avoid mistakes in order to **be acceptable**.

3. I must perform to certain standards to be **loved and accepted** and deserve God's rewards.

4. I must not fail. It would mean **I** *am* **a failure** and **unworthy**.

✓5. I must be in control and "fix" so things won't fall apart. This brings **security** and **approval**.

✓6. Emotions represent truth and can be relied on.

7. I must see to it that I am treated fairly, or with respect, for my **worth to be validated**.

8. I must be heard and/or prove I am right to be assured of my **worth**.

✓9. I am responsible for the emotional well-being of others.

✓10. Others are responsible for my **emotional well-being** or lack of it.

11. I must be best to know I am **of value**.

✓12. I am a reject and without hope. There is no way out of my situation.

13. What I do makes me who I am.

14. I must be the center of attention (things must go my way) to know I am **accepted, of value.**

15. I need a person to **complete and fulfill** me.

16. **Love and acceptance** must be earned.

17. I must be strong and independent and persevere to be **secure** or to **survive.**

18. I am not worthy of **love and acceptance.**

19. I must succeed to overcome my background have **hope, contentment.**

20. **Worth and satisfaction** will come from success, performance and/or others opinions.

21. I can never seem to measure up.

22. I must follow religious rules. They guide me into Christian growth.

23. Maintaining order will bring **contentment, satisfaction.**

24. Things must go my way for me to be **secure, accepted and satisfied.**

25. A job well done should bring **contentment.**

26. I must stay strong and emotionally guarded to be **safe and secure.**

27. Putting myself down or self-pity will bring validation of my **worth.**

28. I must resist being controlled by another to be who I am.

Chapter 6

Lost in the Desert: Going in Circles

> **On the Map:** In the wilderness. The journey continues as we are born-again believers. We bring fleshly myths and behaviors into adulthood and marriage. When we relate out of these old patterns, we wander in circles lost in our own personal wilderness.

The journey continues. We became acquainted with Darryl and Mattie after they moved their baggage out of their early years of survival training and across the Red Sea. When they became believers, they added religious laws and principles to bags already packed with familiar myths and controls. They had entered the desert—the wilderness area of their journeys—where they lived from their own fleshly strategies in vocational and personal relationships.

The baggage became heavier and more burdensome, so breaking down emotionally or getting stuck along the way usually resulted. Somehow though, they had managed to do a few repairs, change a few behaviors and keep going.

The road in the desert can be smooth at times or often quite rough. Our way of thinking and behaving in our marriage relationship seems to be the right way. It is familiar to us and we can't understand why it is not working to bring us what we so desperately need. So, we usually rationalize that it is the other travelers who are causing our problems. At this point we aren't aware that false beliefs or myths are the culprits behind our difficulties.

In the wilderness, most of the time we travel on empty. Nothing we have tried has really filled the vacant spaces. Our efforts to obtain that sense of value and acceptance we long for have been inadequate. The songs that are sung promise completeness and wholeness if we find the right person with whom we can have a relationship. The world is still offering its beguiling anticipations and we believe they are true. Because we are so anxious to find satisfaction and contentment, we are ready for what is next on the road. During this phase of the journey, we come to the place of courtship where we look for a mate who can give us what we need. And here, there is a game to play and it is called, "The Game of the Mythical Mate." Darryl and Mattie were eager to play. And they did.

The Game of the Mythical Mate

In the courtship phase of our trip, we keep most of the stuff we bring hidden in our bags and boxes—except for the masks. For this part of the journey, most of us take out our masks and play a game of pretend. We are led to believe that we play this game so can get what we need for the rest of life's trip.

The game goes like this. We put on our masks and become very compromising. We are magically attracted to what we see of another person who wears a mask and wants to play the game too. Part of the game is that we manufacture a mythical mate out of only the seen and desirable parts of the other person. We create a person who will complete us and meet our needs and who will not challenge us in threatening ways. If we glimpse a part that doesn't fit the person we've manufactured, we must ignore it. *Without realizing it, we may even select the parts of a person that are like the adult with whom we had unresolved issues in those years of our survival training!* When this is the case, we don't realize that we are hoping to get these old issues resolved with a mate so we can finally feel satisfied. We are careful to pretend that our interest is in meeting the other player's needs.

If we play the game successfully, the next move on the journey is to get married. The pastor may tell us that we can expect to get just what we want and need. That is, we won't feel any more loneliness, emptiness, or pain and all our needs will be met. We will then live happily ever after. Now the part that isn't ever told before the wedding is that the mythical mate is only a fantasy person and will disappear after the honeymoon—or sooner. The masks come off. And we realize that our mate is just an ordinary person. When this happens, this particular game is over and one of the hardest parts of the journey begins. So, we settle in and try to find our way with our old survival equipment. This is where we get lost in the wilderness. We hold on to our former ways and keep on doing more of the same while we get more of the same. One reason we continue to live out of old survival strategies is that we haven't heard of another way. Sometimes we stubbornly believe our way is right, regardless. So we get stuck and lost in vicious cycles of relating with our spouse.

The Israelites were lost, wandering in circles in the wilderness for forty years, not understanding, or not willing to see the way out. In the same way, married couples get lost in the desert, struggling and caught in the same defeating, circular patterns year after year, often wondering why they selected that certain spouse. But our attachments are predictable.

Predictable Attachments

It has been said that one reason we attach to a specific marital partner is in an unconscious effort to try to repair childhood hurts. In my years of counseling couples, I have seen validity in this statement. For example, if a person saw a parent or other primary caretaker as smothering, controlling, demanding, difficult, emotionally unavailable, addicted or abusive, and there were unresolved issues with that person, one way to finally find satisfaction is to attach to a person just as difficult and try to work it out—like a delayed replay. And working it out usually means trying to fine approval from the other.

Or, an individual may select someone just the *opposite* of that parent and attempt to find gratification—many years later! In such a case, Mr. "X" may marry a "nice" person and later Mr. "X" may have an affair with someone like the difficult parent to finally try to fill that unmet need from childhood.

However, I believe a person sometimes takes on the characteristics of that controlling or difficult person and still tries to work it out to get needs of acceptance met with another. Regardless, there can be *various reasons* we are attracted to and marry those we do. *What is important to realize is that one marital partner's fleshly strategies do attract to and "hook" with the other's strategies in a predictable way. It is no accident when we become involved with a certain person whose needs are reciprocal to our own.* It is an intermeshing of traits, and rarely are our choices made through random attraction. This means that our mate *seems* to have the qualities we lack or need and that we think will complete us where we are incomplete.

But none of this ever works. When we find the partner we were attracted to resists us, demeans us, ignores us or reasons very differently than we do, we may try to "fix" him or her, or we may decide we made a mistake or that we were deceived. We then become frozen in power struggles, each trying to control or define how the relationship will be lived out (often fighting over the same issues of control as the parents!) This is not surprising, because these styles of relating reflect the ways each tries to extract **Contentment, Security** and **Worth** from the other person. When this is true, the longer we journey with our mate, the more T.I.R.E.D. and lost on our way we become.

Following are some typical combinations of struggling couples. These combinations reflect those predictable attachments. See if you can recognize a pattern of relating in which you and your marital partner may be caught.

Typical Combinations of Marital Partners

*(These and other styles of relating can be combined in various ways.
All represent fleshly strategies or styles of relating.)*

ONE SPOUSE	<=>	OTHER SPOUSE
Emotional guardedness/distancing	<=>	Emotional pursuing/care-taking/"fixing"
One seems empty	<=>	Other seems full
One seems inadequate	<=>	Other seems adequate
Reserved/stoic/logical/steady	<=>	Outgoing/verbose/subjective
Fears decisions/"people-pleaser"	<=>	Dominant/decision-maker/protecting
Abusive/feels entitled	<=>	"Victim"/suspiciousness/helplessness
Perfectionist/organized	<=>	Laid-back/accepting/unorganized
Super responsible	<=>	Irresponsible/sensitive/addictions
Needs to be right/be heard	<=>	Needs to be right/be heard
Frugal/financial security	<=>	Spender/self-indulgent
Independent	<=>	Dependent

**Each spouse's survival strategies tend to "hook" the other's strategies.
We often will marry someone whose strategies will
smother, block, resist, or ignore us.**

While one partner pursues, the other distances, and they are caught in a circular dance that never brings what either wants or needs. Each partner tries, by his/her own strategies, to control how the relationship will be lived out in an effort to meet his/her own needs of **Contentment, Security** and **Worth.**

It is worth noting that the very characteristics we were initially attracted to in our mates are likely the *same* attributes that become sources of conflict later! Think about it. We believed our spouse would help to fill us and make us complete. We believed any differences we acknowledged would be the way we would at least "complement" each other. Or so we had been told. *It turns out that the qualities we thought would be helpful actually seem to be hindrances!*

For example, a partner who is *frugal, reserved* and *steady* and had such a *calming influence* in the beginning, can later be seen as *uninvolved, uncaring, unavailable* and perhaps *"stingy."* The person with the *spontaneous, vibrant personality* who made the reserved partner feel "alive," later may be seen as *unorganized and an irritant* because he/she never stops talking.

The *laid-back, make-no-demands charmer* could turn out *to lie and be irresponsible* or *perhaps abusive* or *addictive*. He works hard to lower others' expectations of him to take the pressure off. If he doesn't try, he can't fail. And, of course, he married the uptight, *super-responsible* one who felt relaxed around his mellow personality. She seemed to complement him so well. But the *responsible* one later becomes *angry and demanding* because of having all the responsibility!

Sometimes *the care-taking, co-dependent* marries one who seems to need "fixing" and who *must be catered-to or rescued in order to feel loved*. The "fixer" believes she knows what is best for others and this justifies her controlling ways. She lives for acceptance and had hoped to get it from pleasing and/or rescuing, but for all her talk about helping and caring, she quickly becomes resentful if she isn't appreciated. She finds these strategies don't work because the partner can never be pleased and only tries to get more.

The dominant decision-maker may marry a *compliant person who is fearful of making decisions or feels helpless in life*. These dominating types may have had a domineering parent, and they need to feel superior to avoid feeling worthless, so they can not risk valuing another's opinions. They aren't threatened by the compliant type, and this individual sometimes uses Scripture to justify his control and the need to be right. While the *compliant* mate initially felt secure with the dominant person, pretty soon he/she feels devalued and ignored and begins to be *resistant.* Conflict ensues.

The *emotional pursuer* marries the *distancer (the emotional isolator)* who fears being known because it might expose his "failure."

There are many combinations of strategies among couples, but each partner in every case is trying to get his/her own needs met by his/her own particular strategies. Each believes the other is at fault when it doesn't happen. It turns out that our manipulations and controls back-fire and do not bring us what we had expected because the focus is on *me, myself and I.* Only circular patterns of disappointment, conflict and pain are our reward. It feels like, and it is, a dry, deserted wilderness.

Each of these individuals is living out of his/her own myths and survival strategies regarding life and marriage. We try to get our spouses to *maintain our myths* by demanding that they comply with our demands! But the consequences are always control, manipulation, false submission and domination. This can involve arguing, hurt, pouting, rage, withdrawing, dependency, irresponsibility, whining, global responsibility, depression, anxiety, physical illness, separation and even divorce.

Following are some of the **Myths of Marriage**. These are typical personal laws or rules we bring into our various spousal combinations. These marital myths serve to keep the cycles of defeating behaviors and damaging emotions going. It may be surprising to learn that these beliefs are erroneous. Check off the myths that apply, or have applied, to you.

Note that the word *entitled* is key when you look at these myths. For example, God *may* command a mate to respond in a certain way, but the other partner is not *entitled* to the mate doing that particular thing and therefore must not demand it nor manipulate to get it! Specific Myths of Marriage will be addressed as we progress through the book and observe couples' struggles in these areas.

Some Myths of Marriage

- ❏ My spouse is to be my completer, otherwise, why marriage?

- ❏ I am entitled to my spouse cherishing me, giving me respect, appreciation, encouragement, listening and…

- ❏ If he/she doesn't, it is destructive to me. I cannot get past this.

- ❏ If we don't verbally communicate about our damaged emotions, we can't have intimacy.

- ❏ I am entitled to my husband being the spiritual leader and assuming his role as head.

- ❏ I am entitled to my wife being submissive and compliant since that is her role.

- ❏ I am entitled to my husband/wife meeting my sexual needs.

- ❏ *Wife*: "If he doesn't, it means I am rejected and I don't measure up."

- ❏ *Husband*: "If she doesn't, or if I can't meet hers, it means I'm not a real man."

- ❏ I am responsible for my partner's emotional well-being, so,

- ❏ I am responsible for seeing to it that he/she is content, that the waters are calmed and for "fixing" (or giving solutions) and making things right because,

- ❏ My peace and emotional well-being is dependent on my spouse and others being okay and on their opinions…and then I will have acceptance and know I am of worth.

- ❏ If I serve my spouse, it makes me a doormat.

- ☑ I need a person (spouse) to be fulfilled, complete, secure, validated.

- ❑ I am entitled to him/her making things okay, making decisions for me and keeping me on track, (so I can avoid being criticized and, thus, avoid being less than perfect).
- ❑ I must be perfect (live to certain standards) so I will be loved by my spouse.
- ☑ My security is to be found in my mate's behaviors (emotional, financial, physical, etc.).
- ❑ If my husband/wife doesn't appreciate me, it means I'm not worthy of love.
- ❑ I am entitled to my husband/wife giving me space to make mistakes, to be my own person without her/him trying to change, criticize or ignore me.
- ❑ Our relationship must be fair and I can't accept that I am not entitled to what the Lord commands my wife/husband to do and be.
- ☑ My unhappiness is the fault of my spouse or my circumstances.
- ❑ It demeans me if my mate criticizes me or tells me what to do.
- ❑ We are wired to find contentment through our work and accomplishments and marriage.
- ❑ I must be in control of circumstances and interactions to remain secure.
- ❑ I am entitled to find contentment by my mate being reasonable, responsible and validating me.
- ❑ I should have the freedom to do what I want.
- ❑ If my mate cares, he/she will intuitively know what I want and need. If I have to ask for it, it won't mean anything.
- ❑ I cannot be content and secure if I can't know my partner is totally trustworthy.

- ❑ The husband is to rule over the wife.
- ❑ If I punish my spouse, he/she will give me what I want and need.
- ❑ We must get attuned to each other to find satisfaction in marriage.
- ❑ The wife is to set the tone for the relationship.
- ❑ I am accountable for my spouse's behavior and spiritual maturity.
- ❑ We become one person at the marriage union.
- ❑ I am entitled to my mate doing what God commands.
- ❑ We must have the same opinions on most things to have intimacy.

BELIEVING MYTHS RESULTS IN:
destructive emotions and *defeating behaviors,*
which can look good *or* bad.

Myths of Marriage
Result in:

DEMANDS,
CONTROL, MANIPULATION,
false submission or domination,

which involve:

↓

Hurt, rage, arguing, whining, pouting,
blame, avoidance, denial, dependency, lying,
unforgiveness, anxiety, hopelessness, depression,
illness, irresponsibility, global responsibility,
separation, divorce.

Chapter 7

Weary Travelers: Tired and Thirsty

> **On the Map:** In the wilderness. Confused couples, holding tightly to heavy baggage, wander in circles in a dry and barren land.

Are we incompatible?

"I think Mattie and I are just incompatible," Darryl growled. "We have found that we just fight the same battles over and over. We don't even have the same interests." The world has identified these defeating patterns and unrelated likes and dislikes as our having "incompatibilities" and "irreconcilable differences."

Archibald Hart, in a speech at an AACC Conference on Marriage in Dallas said,

> God doesn't have the word *incompatibility* in His vocabulary! And it is a given, not the exception, that every marriage relationship is incompatible. Marriage is two imperfect people in an impossible relationship. There is no truth in, "We were intended for each other." Over time, we try to find the beauty of the beginning of the relationship. It wasn't beautiful. You were seeing a "mythical mate." We create fantasy images of the person we desire out of a

few characteristics we are drawn to. We create this delusion to meet our needs. *It is all about us and our getting our needs met.* We must accept that our mate is neither accident nor mistake, but the whole thing is orchestrated by God....

Darryl and Mattie

When I saw Darryl and Mattie as a couple for marital counseling, I learned they had met each other at a singles retreat twelve years before. As time went by, they played "The Game of the Mythical Mate" and married. To their complete surprise, their masks came off a few weeks after the wedding and each felt he/she no longer recognized the other. Consequently, Darryl and Mattie had been in a constant power struggle throughout most of their eleven years of marriage.

In the first counseling session, they sat on opposite ends of my sofa. Each was convinced the other was the problem. Both were hurt, angry and guarded but wanted to save the marriage, so they were willing to open up. Pious and petite Mattie sat up straight with her legs properly crossed at the ankles. She chose her words carefully. Pompous Darryl sat stiffly with his arms *and* legs crossed.

I learned that Mattie had received Christ as a young teenager and Darryl had been a believer since just before they had married. Both were in their late thirties and attended church rather frequently. In their understanding, religion was a lot of "dos" and "don'ts," and each believed the other wasn't living up to what Scripture requires of a spouse.

Mattie stated the difficulty was Darryl's refusal to take responsibility and his resistance to being involved with her and the kids. She felt that he wasn't providing financially in his role as husband. Since he had withdrawn into his own interests, Mattie felt alone, without any companionship. She found herself angry over having all the responsibility for making decisions and carrying them out. She revealed, "None of my needs are being met. I feel shut out and not appreciated. He never listens to me. He always has to be right. I just need his reassurance that I am valuable and loved by him. All I want is to be cherished by Darryl, but he gets defensive and caustic and withdraws from me for days."

Darryl was aloof when he expressed how tired he was of a marriage where all he heard was yelling and criticism. He admitted, "Sometimes, I lose my temper, but it is because of the constant nagging. The problem is that Mattie wants everything done in her way and in her time. She is nosy about everyone's business. Furthermore, she interrupts, corrects, answers questions directed at others and talks over them. She tries to fix and orchestrate things for me. She thinks she is being nice, but it is on *her* terms and not what I want. Then she says I don't love or appreciate her. She does this with all her family. I feel the same way about her as she does about me. She never regards *me* and what *I* want. I can't do anything right. She blames me and contests me on everything. I don't want to have to defend everything."

He growled, "At this point all I want is some peace and some space. I work my job, but my paycheck is never enough for her. If she would only give me some peace and appreciation and get off my back! I do the best I can. I know my income is low right now and we're having to use some money she inherited and she resents it. I can't stand any more of her nips and complaining."

Darryl and Mattie were stuck in a repetitive cycle of her pursuing and his withdrawing. Their goal for counseling was for me to give them some biblical principles and communication skills to enhance their marriage. Each wanted me to get the other to change. They were surprised and a little let down at first when I told them that the issues they presented were symptoms of the true problem. I explained that because of our counseling perspective, I would not give a list of "dos" and "don'ts" for their relationship. This would only address behavior change, which, in itself, never lasts and would lead to more demands.

Undesirable behaviors and emotions are the fruit produced by myths or wrong beliefs. If we focus primarily on behavior modification such as managing the anger or enhancing communication, it is like cutting fruit off a vine and more defective fruit will grow back if the root of wrong thinking is not identified and changed. *Transformation of each individual's mind-set had to begin before the issues could be resolved. Skills-building can be great, but not until the underlying problem is dealt with.*

I described our process of counseling, which is based on grace and knowing Christ as their life and sufficiency. I told them they were on a journey and I would be walking with them as they found the way out of their personal wilderness. I explained that I would help identify false beliefs they had brought into the relationship and then they would learn to replace these myths with truth in their marriage. Darryl and Mattie were relieved and excited to be given some direction and hope for their relationship.

After hearing the background of their conflicts, I took personal histories of each while the other listened. The histories helped identify the patterns of relating they developed early in life and brought into adulthood. These patterns included those wrong beliefs about God, themselves, and how emotional needs should be satisfied within relationships.

Darryl's and Mattie's beliefs were not grace-oriented but performance-based. Each believed he must perform for God and measure up to the partner's standards to know he was acceptable. If one of them didn't *feel* accepted, it confirmed the myth that he or she was a loser. Both believed they were entitled to fairness and respect and tried to hurt the other when it wasn't forthcoming. Even though they expressed it in different ways, both of them felt the need to control interactions to find approval and protect themselves emotionally. Anger and hurt lay hidden under all of their behaviors—in *her* perfectionism and emotional pursuit of Darryl and in *his* withdrawing and irresponsibility. This vicious cycle had lasted for years.

Each began to relax and drop their guardedness as they listened to the partner's history. Both saw that the spouse's behaviors and bitter responses were caused by beliefs about meeting needs that were *brought into the marriage!* They began to see each other differently.

After taking their histories, I charted each partner's myths and defeating behaviors. I do not analyze; I only gave feedback on what they had revealed about themselves. Darryl and Mattie were receptive and amazed when they saw these patterns in "black and white."

In the chapter on survival strategies I presented a little of Darryl's and Mattie's individual histories and the myths they had developed. When I gave them the "Myths of Marriage" sheet to look over, the couple was very surprised to learn that most of what they believed they were *entitled to* in marriage were *false beliefs*.

I will re-visit Mattie and Darryl and show how they walked, often struggling, through the rest of their journey to find victory and healing in Christ. As we progress through the next chapters, this spiritual perspective will unfold.

Darryl and Mattie were still exhausted and confused, not knowing the way out of their wilderness and the repetitive series of conflicts. They were weary travelers, tired and thirsty, but *their thirst couldn't be quenched by all their best efforts to get the other to give what they needed.* They didn't know yet the truth contained in Arch Hart's words, or the truth that would calm troubled waters, quench their thirst and set them free.

Are We Incompatible?

Archibald Hart, in a speech at the 2000 AACC Conference on Marriage in Dallas said, "God doesn't have the word *incompatibility* in His vocabulary! And it is a given, not the exception, that every marriage relationship is incompatible." Hart described marriage as "Two imperfect people in an impossible relationship." He said, "There is no truth in, 'We were intended for each other.'"

He added, "Over time, we try to find the beauty of the beginning of the relationship. It wasn't beautiful. You were seeing a "mythical mate." We create fantasy images of the person we desire out of a few characteristics we are drawn to. We create this delusion to meet our needs. It is all about us and our getting our needs met." He went on to say, "We must accept that our mate is neither accident nor mistake, but the whole thing is orchestrated by God…"

Chapter 8

Found: Water and New Information

On the Map: In the wilderness. Couples discover new information and new directions pointing to the way out of a dry and barren land.

When I was five or six, sometimes I went with my dad out past our apple trees and the bed of rose bushes, through the neighbor's gate by the chinaberry tree where I watched him draw water for our cow. We kept her over there in Mr. Oxford's vacant pasture by the barn and abandoned, but once grand, antebellum house. As I carefully leaned over the three-foot high side of the gray wooden well, there was the distinctive musty scent of damp red clay. There was a reflecting pool of water at the bottom.

The wood creaked and squeaked as the rope that was securely wound around the log windlass quickly let the bucket down to be filled. My dad slowly cranked it back up as it groaned under the weight of the heavy load. Resting the large metal container on the side of the well, he tipped it so I could sip the cool, clear liquid.

The woman at the well had five husbands. She had looked to find completeness in a husband. She had looked to men to quench her thirst for love, worth and fulfillment. Jesus met up with her at the well and said in effect, "I will fill you and make you complete. If you drink of my living water, you will never thirst nor crave for validation and satisfaction from a person again." If we drink of Jesus Christ—water that is running and bubbling and a well that will never run dry—we will be filled and fulfilled.

Charles Stanley said that God never intended that we live unfulfilled, nor did He ever intend that we find fulfillment in a person, our performance or personality! Believers can *have* Christ's indwelling life (the Holy Spirit) and yet not *experience* this life fully, nor *feel* complete, because they are still looking to experience it from the wrong source.

There may be times that we feel a cool satisfying sip of water on our tongue when we get kudos or get our mate or another person to give us what we long for, but it never lasts. Darryl and Mattie had experienced that very thing. Each was struggling to find validation and peace from the other, and they were left thirsty.

That sly fox!

It is Satan's trickery that hooks us into thinking we can be satisfied by people, personality or performance—that we can drink from those sources and our thirst will finally be quenched. But what happens is that it only creates more and more thirst—AND more and more conflict as we react out of false hope! We are tempted to try to satisfy our emptiness by hollow promises and beguiling anticipations that can't deliver.

Satan can only cause devastation in believers by deceiving them. That is why we urgently need to know the truth that will set us free from our old strategies and that will quench our thirst. We must realize that if we are caught up in circular patterns of defeat in our marriage relationship, we are believing lies, and there is truth we must learn.

Cackle, cackle!! squawk, squawk!! cluck, cluck, squawk, clip, clip!!! We were awakened in the middle of a July night by the sound of a dozen hens in crisis. Many wings were fluttering in an effort to protect themselves and their territory in the hen house. My dad's quick steps were heard as he went down the hall and out the back door. Shortly, he returned. Hearing the slam of the screen door, I asked what was wrong. He only replied, "A fox got in the hen house."

Jesus called Satan, "That sly fox." He tricks us into believing our old ways and beliefs are valid and that happiness should come from performance and people—especially our marital partners. Even though our old strategies haven't worked, he uses the media and all those beguiling anticipations to deceive us into thinking they will. *He even uses religious rules and principles to trick us.* If we have never understood God's grace, we are still thinking we must perform to please God, ourselves, or other people to find acceptance, worth and be absolved of guilt.

Darryl and Mattie at the well

It was about their seventh counseling session. Mattie's Christmas sweater perfectly complemented my burgundy and green sofa. They still sat on opposite ends of it. Darryl leaned forward and expressed enthusiasm over what they had learned concerning their old patterns of thinking and behaving. Each was becoming aware of why the other believed and reacted the way he/she did in the relationship. They were still hurting, but there was a softening of their caustic attitudes toward each other.

Even though both were beginning to be hopeful in counseling, Mattie continued to express her discouragement over feeling all the responsibility in the marriage without being appreciated in return. She related how she was trying a lot of religious things to find Christ in the midst of her disappointment.

"I've focused on simplifying and having my quiet times and really centering on my participation in my weekly Scripture study group." She explained, "I've tried to keep a balanced view on a beautiful home and my marriage, but my emotions aren't lining up. My husband is still the same. I am not finding what I believe should be finding in my marriage. It's all just so painful."

I encouraged them that we were on track in their learning process and they could look forward to discovering truths that would counteract the myths we had found in their personal baggage. They would learn Scriptures about God's grace, their identity in Christ and how they were created to relax rather than struggle. Believe it or not, this would have a tremendous bearing on the marriage.

Since I knew that Darryl and Mattie were steeped in misunderstandings about their relationship to God and living the Christian life, I assigned the first half of the book, *Grace Walk* by Steve McVey. The book would fit perfectly with what they needed in the counseling process. It would help them begin to understand these truths so that in time they could renew their thinking.

Found: Water and new information!

Darryl and Mattie were faithful in keeping each appointment on time. However, the next week they were early. Darryl's excited response to the past week's assignment of *Grace Walk* was, "This is so different than anything we have been taught about ourselves as believers and the Christian walk. I am eager to learn more. You know I have been "set" in some of my religious views. *The book reveals that we have been living under law rather than God's grace!* It will take time to change my understanding and to learn what this has to do with marriage."

Not only this couple but many others who attend church and Bible study groups have some erroneous religious beliefs. Darryl and Mattie were mixing these ideas with their personal myths about marriage and the outcome was disaster. They were ready for water, a new map and new information to guide them out of the wilderness.

Both had concluded early in life that love, acceptance and good things must be earned from God and others. Each secretly felt unacceptable and struggled to prove worth by personal sets of "dos" and don'ts" (laws). Yet, never feeling they measured up, each was emotionally guarded and looked for rejection from God and the other. In addition, each believed the pain would go away if the *other* would comply with their set of expectations (laws)!

Steve McVey says that most religious people are trying to score brownie points with God. They have been given the idea that because they have been born again, they (and the mate) have to fulfill a duty to God by religious performance. Nothing could be farther from the truth, because we were not created to *do* but to *be*. God's grace allows us to *be* and to enjoy God and His provision in life and relationships. It allows us to know Him and this is to enjoy eternal life! (John 17:3).

Unless we know *who* we have become as new creations, being *one with Christ*—our spirit joined with His Spirit and infused with Divine life—we cannot just relax and *be*. We just keep *struggling* to *do* and *demand* from others to find acceptance and satisfy our thirst for those needs of *Contentment*, *Security* and *Worth* to be met. Nowhere is that more evident than in marriage.

I began teaching Darryl and Mattie about God's grace and their worth and acceptance in Christ, which paralleled what they were reading. Before we could proceed in counseling, they needed to understand that Christ came to give *His life* to indwell them without any conditions attached. As most Christians, the couple believed that they were born again by grace through faith, but after that they had to struggle to *do* the best they could to get what they needed and wanted.

They really had not known exactly *what* happened at their new birth. I would tell them, and in doing so, I would describe their make-up as individuals. They learned that as humans, *we are spirit, soul and body (1 Thessalonians 5:23; Hebrews 4:12). We are **spirit** persons who have a **soul** containing our mind, beliefs and emotions. In Scripture, the **soul** often means our personality or heart. And we live in a **body**. The **body** is the house (temple) in which our **spirit** lives (John 3:6; Ephesians 2:5; 1 Corinthians 2:13). The **Spirit** is the power source that empowers the mind to think, the will to choose, the emotions to feel and the body to move.* Scripture says that without the **Spirit**, the **Body** is dead.

I recounted to Darryl and Mattie the story of Adam's and Eve's disobedience and how we inherited neediness and a spirit empowered by sin. Because we are *spirit* people, sin was *who we were*. It was our very nature. So before we were born of God, sin empowered our every thought, choice and conclusion even though much of what we did looked great and reasoned out to be right! Our sin nature empowered our childhood solutions and helped form our old belief system about how needs should be met. These beliefs or myths are in our *soul* and are lived out through the *body*—the areas of our fleshly strategies.

These concepts are often pictured as three concentric circles. Illustrations of spirit, soul and body are provided on the pages entitled,

"Illustration of a Person in Adam: Spirit, Soul and Body" and "Illustration of a Believer Walking After the Flesh: Spirit, Soul and Body" to help you visualize these truths.

Water!

The good news is that at our new birth, Christ not only forgave all of our past, present and future sins, He also did something else astounding. He took away and *crucified our sin nature* that was located in our spirit. He crucified *who we were* (Romans 6:7-8) and gave us His nature—His Spirit and His life—to indwell our *new spirit! We became new creations* (1 Corinthians 5:17), *united with Him and one Spirit with Him* (1 Corinthians 6:17). *This is an actual fact.* It does not just exist in God's mind. It is not "just the way He sees us." What happened was that our sin nature and our separation from God *died* on the cross. Galatians 2:20 says that we were *crucified with Christ;* nevertheless we live. Yet, it is not we who live, but it is Christ in us!

If we have received Christ, who we *were* died. And we were born again into God's family. We were placed into Christ (1 Corinthians 1:30; Colossians 3:3). Our new *spirit* is united with the *eternal nature and life of Christ,* which is holy, perfect and righteous (Romans 8:11). Satan's trick is *to deceive us into believing that what we do or feel makes us who we are.* The truth is *we are who we are by birth.* Birth determines our identity.

Christ dwells in us as the Holy Spirit (2 Timothy 1:14; 1 Corinthians 3:11; Romans 8:9; Ezekiel 36:26; Colossians 1:27). We are in Him and He is in the Father. We are all safely sealed up together! (John 14: 20). God has made us as accepted and as righteous as we will ever be in our *spirit* (Christ in us) (Ephesians 4: 6; 2 Corinthians 5:21). Colossians 2:10 says each of us been made complete in Him. We no longer need to struggle to *be* something we already *are.* Scripture refers to us as saints, holy and accepted.

Christ in us has become our new and perfect Source of power and provision—our life! He is the Source of our **Contentment, Security,** our **Worth** and everything else we need, (Philippians 4:19) even though we may not have *experienced* this yet. He is able to do abundantly beyond all we could ask or think according to the power that works in us as new creations (Ephesians 3:20). We can do all things through Christ who strengthens us (Philippians 4:13). We have been set free from the power of the sin nature over our attitudes and behavior, and Scripture says we are to consider that to be fact. Our *feelings* may tell us otherwise, *but negative emotions do not represent truth since they are consequences of our old thinking.*

We have been made the righteousness of God (2 Corinthians 5:21) in our *spirit*. But the problem is that the old programming (myths) still remains in our *soul* and, as a result, our behaviors aren't always holy. When we sin and walk after the old myths and emotions in our *soul*, these old fleshly ways *block* the life of Christ within us from flowing out and being experienced by ourselves and others. They are like the chaff covering a grain of wheat or like putting a basket over a light, preventing the life or light from flowing out.

If we do not embrace these truths, we continue to seek to fill our neediness by behavior and externals. We still live out of others' opinions of us and try to make them comply with our demands so they will fill us and complete us. *The Scripture refers to this as our walking after the flesh.* It doesn't work because Christ in us is the water that will quench our thirst.

The journey out of the wilderness includes our being transformed in our *soul*. This happens by renewing our minds to line up with the mind of Christ that indwells our *spirit* and yielding our old independent strategies up to Him. Our emotions may not line up immediately, but they will when we choose to believe and act on the truth as we live and relate with others—especially our mates. This is when we choose to *walk after the Spirit*.

I briefly related to Darryl and Mattie how their journey is like that of the Children of Israel from Egypt to Canaan. Mattie's response was, "Nobody told us what had happened to us when we were born again— when we crossed the Red Sea. We didn't know that we have Christ's life and all of His provision within in us and that His identity is our identity. You seem to be saying that we have been living as if we were still in captivity in Egypt, when we are really free! I don't understand what all of this means for us in overcoming our conflicts and leaving the desert we find ourselves in.

This is such new information and really different thinking. How can it become a reality in our lives? What does it have to do with marriage?"

"Mattie, the purpose of the remainder of your counseling will be my helping you to experience these truths in your relationship with each other," I replied.

Our culture demands success and personal strength. Weakness is never acceptable. Darryl and Mattie, as most Christians, knew they were "saved" to go to heaven but saw themselves as without power and unacceptable unless they kept up good performance. My desire was that they would know Christ set them free from having to measure up to any religious or personal rules and from the condemnation that comes with that thinking. I wanted them to drink the water that would quench their thirst as they lived in relationship to each other.

Following are visual illustrations of the concepts to which I have been referring. I use concentric circles to represent *spirit*, *soul* and *body*. The first diagram, "Illustration of a Person in Adam: Spirit, Soul and Body," depicts an individual still living under the power of the old sin nature. The second diagram, "Illustration of a New Creation: Spirit, Soul and Body," describes a person who has been born again but who is still walking after the fleshly strategies. Study them for yourself and refer to them occasionally as we follow our couples on their journeys.

Illustration of a Person in Adam:
Spirit, Soul and Body

The three concentric circles represent a person. A person is made up of *spirit, soul* and *body*. The *spirit* is the basic nature of a person—it identifies *who* we are and *what empowers us* to live, think and behave. The *soul* contains the person's mind, beliefs and emotions. The *body* is the temple or house we live in. When we were in Egypt, before our new birth, our basic nature and identity—the thing that empowered us and held us captive—was sin. We were sinful throughout our *spirit, soul* and *body*. This is an illustration of us when we were held under the captivity of sin and when we drew conclusions about what would make life work for us. Many of our survival strategies were formed at this time. This is when we were *walking in the flesh* (Romans 7:5 KJV).

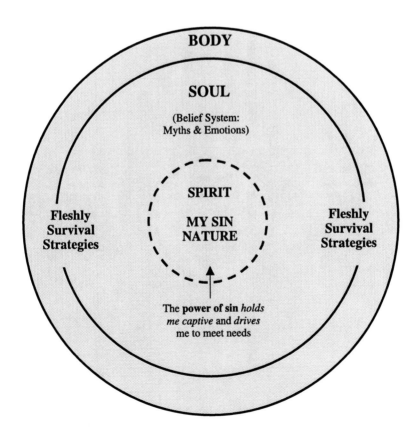

Illustration of a New Creation Walking After the Flesh: *Spirit, Soul and Body*

When we crossed the Red Sea, or were born again, our old sin nature died with Christ. We were given a new spirit. Christ's perfect Spirit came to indwell our *spirit*. His holy and perfect nature replaced our sinful nature, and we became one Spirit with Him! We are empowered by the Spirit of Christ and have a new identity. We were no longer held captive by sin.

However, our *soul* still contains the baggage of old strategies from Egypt. Scripture calls this baggage "flesh." Although we are no longer *in* the flesh, we can still live *after the flesh*, out of our old ways in the areas of our *soul* and *body*. When we live from our myths—our old survival strategies—Scripture says this is like our putting a bushel over the light (Christ) in our spirit. Our old ways are like the chaff covering a grain of wheat. They are also like those *weeds* that choke the Word from being profitable. As long as we *walk after the flesh*, we block our experience of the good things God has already given us in the person of Christ!

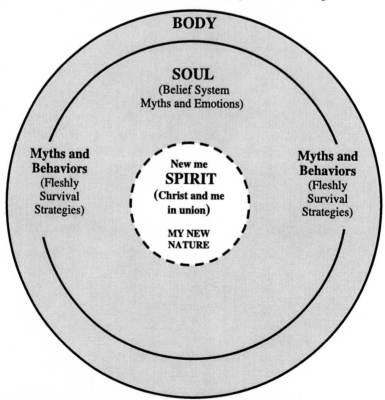

Chapter 9

More Couples: Stranded

> **On the Map:** In the wilderness. More couples struggle, not understanding grace and truth.

A couple, Tony and Katrina, and another couple, Latoya and Joe, were in counseling at approximately the same time as Darryl and Mattie. I am introducing these two couples, who were also stranded and struggling with bitter disappointments, so you can observe how three couples' journeys out of the wilderness are each unique. You will see how all but one partner found the way out and into God's freedom and fulfillment.

Tony and Katrina

Tony was stocky, brunette and sun-tanned. Soft brown eyes smiled from behind gold-rimmed glasses. He was friendly and reminded me of a teddy bear. He was casual and wore boots to the sessions since he came from his job as project manager on high-rise construction downtown. His red shirt had the company logo on it. Tony's comments were free and easy as he sat with his arm across the back of my sofa. But he could become teary, sulk and be accusing and demanding of Katrina when he was hurt.

Katrina was tall and thin and wore her tailored slacks beautifully. To see her delicate, porcelain-like complexion, carefully applied makeup, cropped dark brown hair and hoop earrings, one might not suspect that she was seething with anger—except when she stared at her lap, crossed her long arms and legs and jiggled her foot. Her blue eyes rarely made contact with me or Tony.

Both Tony and Katrina had been married once before to other mates with whom they had grown children. Sexual difficulty was the issue that prompted them to come for counseling, and it was the focus of their power struggle. Couples always have surface issues by which each mate's root problems (flesh) are expressed. It is in these power struggles that each partner attempts to define (control) how the relationship will be lived out.

Most couples have sexual problems as part of their major counseling concerns—whether they reveal this or not. Tony felt he was too often being denied what he considered his sexual right in marriage. Since her kids were adults, Katrina worked a late shift on her nursing job. Caring for her patients had recently evolved into her staying after hours and getting home too late to spend time with Tony. Her time off usually revolved around her children.

Tony said in his gravelly voice, "I really want to save the marriage, but Katrina must change sexually and do more things around the house."

Katrina's voice was always terse. She said that she also wanted to save it, if *he* would change. Her angry comments were biting. "His mother slights me and hates my guts. I have no use for her. She never asks about me. His family doesn't care about me. I have a right for him to protect me from them. He lies to me about the money he gives his kids. He's focused on bailing them out of continual problems. I need to know I can trust him. I am not willing to make it work if this doesn't change. He totally disregards *me and my emotions*. We cannot connect and have any intimacy unless he is willing to value my feelings and share his also."

Tony said, "Her mother catered to her and she never learned to do any housework. She isn't organized and things stay a mess. Whatever is done, including cooking, I have to do it. And yet she never has time for sex."

Katrina retorted, "It's because I am in a helping profession with patients that I just can't walk out on at a certain time. They need me. I

78

must also oversee others during late shift hours, and you know it!"

I informed them, "If marriage counseling is to be successful, both of you will have to agree you want the relationship to work, and each of you must be willing to take an honest look at what *you* are contributing to your problem." I described the counseling process and noted that it cannot be based on one's goal of the other changing. Katrina exclaimed, "But we've been told all our lives that the things we seek are to be found in marriage and we can expect God to give it to us through our marital partners." She was holding on to one of the beguiling anticipations that we learn early in life.

Unlike Tony and Katrina, often when couples come for counseling, they tell me they are willing to invest anything to save the marriage. **I tell them that it is not *the marriage* that must be transformed, but *themselves*.**

Tony and Katrina professed to be Christians and attended church regularly. Eventually they agreed they wanted to go through counseling and wanted to know the truth about themselves and what a godly marriage is. The couple was curious about what would transpire, but there were struggles and resistances in the first few weeks. Gradually, as each presented his/her own personal history and recognized some survival strategies and ways of trying to manipulate the other for protection and worth, the anger was diffused.

When they realized that the patterns were brought *into* the marriage, Katrina relaxed and began to make more eye-contact. Her foot jiggled less. But she still never smiled.

I learned that Tony grew up with supportive parents. His mother was always there to take care of his needs while his father worked long hours to provide for the family. When they were teenagers, Tony and his brother were hired by their strong, demanding father and learned the value of hard work. Their father gave them the view that they must demand respect from a wife and employees to know their value as men.

Evidence to Tony that he was cared about and of worth was having a wife who would keep a clean house, have dinner on the table when he came home and provide sex on demand. Tony was getting none of this. His frustration showed.

Katrina's father had been demanding and abusive to her in her growing-up years. Her mother was a fearful people-pleaser who tried to keep him calm. She catered to Katrina out of pity for her. Consequently, Katrina had lived the life of a victim, feeling powerless and believing she was worthless. As a result she learned to be very guarded, and the reason was, "So others won't see who I really am." She believed she should be perfect to gain acceptance from others, but since she could not be perfect in *her* eyes, she read the actions of others as rejecting and threatening.

Peggy Noonan, in her book, *When Character Was King,* aptly said that so many of the big decisions we make in life we make in childhood, and we don't even know we are making them. Because children often make decisions to protect themselves without knowing it, so many of our learned defenses aren't known to us or deliberate when we become adults.

When Tony and Katrina inspected the trunks and bags they had brought into adulthood and into this dry, barren wilderness, they discovered *both* were living out some of the same myths such as:

- I am not acceptable.
- I am entitled to respect by my mate, to know I am of **value**.
- I am entitled to my spouse making me feel **complete, fulfilled**.

Katrina's false beliefs also included:

- I must be perfect to be **loved** and **know I am of worth**.
- I must please others to be **loved** and **accepted**, but there is no way I can.
- Emotions represent truth and can be relied on.
- I must stay guarded to **be safe, secure**.

A couple of Tony's other myths were:

- My **value as a man** is determined by my mate's sexual response.
- My **contentment** is dependent on my mate's performance.
- Things must go my way for me to feel **important and of worth**.

Counseling helped to make Tony and Katrina aware of their old strategies, including these myths, so they eventually could choose against relying on them. They recognized that they were trying to extract worth and acceptance from each other in different ways. While Tony was demanding and accusing, Katrina had a victim identity and whined, sniped and emotionally withdrew. Tony pursued emotionally and Katrina distanced emotionally. They saw that their difficulties were much deeper than the presenting problems. Being faced with some of their fleshly strategies, each cautiously said they wanted to learn about Christ meeting their needs even though all of that was puzzling at this point.

So I introduced them to the truths of grace and their identity in Christ. I used some visual illustrations to help communicate these concepts, and they seemed to be captivated by this new information. They began to hear that *what they were so desperately seeking from each other is provided in Christ.* I sent a table entitled, "Myths vs Truth" home with them so they could begin to renew their thinking by referring to it each day and comparing their myths with contrasting scriptural truths.

After studying the chart for a week, Tony returned to counseling and said, "It will certainly take a while to change my thinking to my being complete in Christ and to Him being the Source of my fulfillment. That is hard to accept knowing my emotions and thinking have never lined up with that." I assured them it takes time for everyone.

They were having difficulty believing they had actually become new creations with new identities. Katrina's response to the truths I had presented was doubt. "It is hard to receive that all the bad things I did don't matter anymore. And it is hard to accept that all that has happened to me and the emotions I live with don't have to control me anymore," she said.

Katrina would need real encouragement to receive more fully the Lord's forgiveness. She needed support in learning that neither what happened to her early in life, nor her performance, nor what Tony did or thought, *made her who she is*! Rather she is a new creation, righteous and secure in Christ. In time, Katrina would have to learn to make deliberate decisions to trust God for her emotional safety in her relationships, especially marriage.

We will revisit Tony and Katrina from time to time as they proceed on their journey. We will see how their walk together was often precarious but how, in time, it led to freedom and victory in Christ.

Latoya and Joe

When Latoya and Joe came to their first counseling session, they sat stiffly across from me with their dark eyes averted. They were polished and had beautiful, dark golden-brown complexions—like coffee and cream.

Latoya's black hair was pulled tightly back in a bun. She had come from work at a technology firm in a conservative, purple business suit. Latoya sat stiffly on the edge of the sofa. She held her head high and spoke unhesitatingly and with purpose. She was nice but serious.

Joe's bright tropical shirt was neatly tucked in black pants that cuffed across his shiny patent shoes. He was guarded as he crossed his legs and clasped his hands together across his chest and glanced around the ceiling. He looked at his watch a lot. Joe spoke softly and only when I asked him a question, but I learned he had a job in customer service with a discount store. At first, both insisted all they wanted and needed from counseling was better communication skills and more agreement on decision-making. Since I have been counseling for years, I knew there were more issues. And there were.

Latoya finally revealed that she suspected Joe was having an affair, and her main goals were to be able to know she could trust Joe completely and for him to take more responsibility in the family. Each agreed there were sexual problems. Latoya said, "I don't believe I can ever be content or have any peace as long as I do not have complete confidence in knowing Joe will never stray. Furthermore, he is beginning to be abusive." She was angry and depressed, yet controlled.

I learned that Joe had come to counseling only because of an ultimatum given him by Latoya that he go with her or else. Joe insisted that there was no affair. He said, "My complaint is that Latoya makes all the decisions and controls everything. If I try to do anything, I get criticized." He lamented, "My input doesn't count at all with Latoya." I later discovered that since Joe's teen years, he had been irresponsible and angry. He had battled with self-esteem and control problems that manifested in abusive rage, defensiveness, impulsiveness and a sexual addiction.

During their history-taking sessions, I found that Latoya saw her growing-up years as times of poverty and oppression. Her father had left when she was four years old. Her mother had worked two jobs to support her and her sister while her aunts and other extended family helped in raising the girls. Over time, Latoya revealed, "I learned early that I must buck-up and take it, stuff emotions, be strong and in control of all aspects of my life if I wanted to be secure and escape my oppressive background." Latoya had become independent and persevering to survive and had looked to attain worth by success as an officer with the technology company.

Early in her counseling, Latoya didn't realize that even though we develop strategies to compensate for our background, we do not emotionally escape our backgrounds by our very best coping mechanisms! Latoya was typical of strong, super-responsible individuals who come into marriage and are resentful that the partner does not take more responsibility and value them more. Ironically, because of her control and independence, she couldn't receive even if those things were given!

Joe had also grown up in circumstances of poverty and rejection. He revealed, "My father left when I was fourteen. It was after years of alcohol abuse and conflict with my mother. I have never been able to get past my resentment of him leaving us." Joe considered his father's leaving a personal rejection. His mother was the strong, persevering bread-winner who took care of the family and, without realizing it, rescued the boys from having to experience the consequences of their actions. Even though Joe was a sensitive man, he saw himself as a loser and expressed that he felt he had been prevented by his father, by his circumstances and by Latoya from having what he wanted and needed.

It isn't surprising that Joe married someone much like his mother and that Latoya's attraction was to a man who was similar to her father.

Joe had learned early to go into his own fantasy world of pornography and alcohol to escape the pain and responsibilities of life. Latoya revealed that she had accidentally found pornography in the house and Joe confessed to being involved with it since he was a teenager. A few weeks into counseling, he finally admitted to Latoya that he had been caught looking at porn on the Internet at his job in customer service and had actually been suspended for several days.

Joe's myths included:

- I am a loser.
- I am not capable of rising above my situation.
- Being rescued means I am **cared about and of value.**

- I am entitled to others covering my mistakes.

- I must have a "place" where I can **avoid stress** and **be safe**.

Among Latoya's myths were:

- I must be in control to **survive and be secure**.

- I must be independent to **be secure**.

- I must be super-responsible for my family to **be secure** and to affirm my **value**.

- I must be strong, buck-up and take it and persevere for me and my family to escape poverty and oppression and find **security and worth**.

- I must accomplish and be the best to prove I am **of worth**.

Latoya and Joe needed to understand the truths of identity, acceptance, worth and security *in Christ*. .Both needed to know that they could find completeness and fulfillment without their familiar controls and survival strategies. They needed to better understand God's forgiveness. They also needed to see the Lord's purpose in allowing a mate's imperfections and oppositions in the relationship.

Joe was not a Christian even though he went to church with Latoya when she insisted. Even though Latoya had been taken to church as a child, she had only recently received Christ. She was a new believer and had much to learn. Latoya commented, "My mother saw to it that we were all in church on many Sundays, but Joe has rarely been to church." Latoya also had some wrong beliefs about Christianity.

Latoya and Joe had helped me learn about their backgrounds and their survival strategies—the patterns they had developed in attempts to stay safe and find worth. But when I began teaching truth and how it contrasted with the myths they had developed, Joe was skeptical of the message of God's forgiveness and his identity in Christ and was not interested in continuing counseling. He dropped out.

Latoya was tired, hurting and resentful from trying to get Joe to change. After considering Joe's decision to discontinue, Latoya said, "I believe from what little I know about your counseling model that you will help lead me into God's truth. I know it will take time, but I don't know what alternative I have. Based on what you have said, if I leave Joe, I could get involved in another relationship of the same kind if I haven't come into some healing and learn how to live from Christ as my Source." I was glad she was open to learning truth and finding freedom in Christ. I had explained early in counseling our spiritual perspective and the journey we would take.

I have mentioned this couple to illustrate how one partner can find victory in Christ—while living within the marriage relationship—regardless of whether the mate changes or continues to participate in counseling. I will occasionally refer to Latoya's progress in the following chapters since I take individuals through a similar counseling process as couples. I disciple each person in how Christ's life is to be lived out in his or her relationships.

Chapter 10

Myths and Laws vs. Grace and Truth: A Struggle in the Wilderness

> **On the Map:** In the wilderness. Struggling to understand law and grace.

Darryl, Mattie and grace

Pious and proper Mattie still sat with her ankles crossed and her hair hooked behind one ear. Crisply pressed and erudite Darryl still pontificated at times while they were learning truths of their identity in Christ versus erroneously looking to each other to give what only the Lord provides.

When we contrasted Darryl and Mattie's myths about how their needs should be met with the truths of needs being met in Christ, it was eye-opening. Each had been trying unsuccessfully to extract from performance, religious activity and each other those things that would fulfill and satisfy.

Darryl lamented, "But *others* DO accept us based on our performance or personality." He said, "Believing these truths will be an entirely different way of thinking for me. Depending on Christ for my emotional protection will be totally unfamiliar. I've never heard anything like this." Since Darryl had such ingrained patterns of emotionally withdrawing to feel safe, it would indeed be a different way of relating.

Neither would look at me nor at the other. Darryl shifted his position closer to his arm of the sofa, crossed his legs away from Mattie and me, and said, "In spite of everything you are telling us, I still have many doubts about being able to stay in the marriage if she doesn't change." I had explained to them in the beginning that the purpose of counseling would not be to change the other person. At this point things became quiet.

Mattie finally spoke, "I'm still a little incredulous. We've never heard anything like the things you're teaching us." Then she asked, "But what do I do about my *emotions?* I am so hurt because Darryl doesn't cherish me. I need to feel valued. I don't know how to receive that from Christ!" I assured her that, in time, I would explain how to live beyond emotions and she would experience the Lord meeting those needs.

Darryl and Mattie had not understood God's grace and that *in Him* we have already been *freely given* all things to enjoy that pertain to life and godliness. They did not know *how to experience* what had already been given them in Christ. We will follow them as they make these discoveries.

Darryl revealed, "I have never known just what *grace* is or what a scriptural marriage is supposed to look like. Can you help me learn?" I enthusiastically replied, "Yes!" *Amazing Grace.* The thought took me back.

I was five years old. The summer was stifling and the pew was damp from my perspiration. I had just been awakened from my dream by my mother fanning away a housefly that had found its way into the open window of the white-frame church. A picture of Jesus and the children was on the flip side of the cardboard fan with a wooden handle that advertised Haisten's Funeral Home, Barnesville, Ga.

Suddenly, the shiny oak floors and pews creaked and bumped under the shuffle of the congregation rising to sing strains of, "A-ma-zing grace, how sweet th' sound, that saved a wretch li-ke me-e...I once was lost, but now am found, was blind, but n-ow I see-e...." Miss Minnie's shrill soprano and Mr. Grady's deep bass were comfortably familiar as they rang out above the rest. Even though I didn't know what it meant until many years later, the song always somehow made me feel secure and comfortable. I'm not sure everyone else understood it either.

Grace, law and the struggle

Today I *know* that trying to live by religious laws and regulations—or by *my own* myths and laws—instead of by grace and truth will only bring struggles, defeat and death to my relationships. I remarked to Darryl and Mattie that even the Ten Commandments, God's holy law, were called the "law of *sin and death*"! Scripture tells us that the very power behind our sin and failure is *the law* (1 Corinthians 15:56) When we try to live by our own rules or religious laws and make demands on others to live by them, it brings forth sin and results in anger in our relationships (Romans 4:15). It results in our being separated from God's best.

For believers, Christ was an end of the law being a means of our acceptance with God. When I explained that the law is made for the lawless, not Christians, Mattie exclaimed, "What did you say? That will take some time to soak in! Show us where that is in Scripture."

Looking stunned, Darryl unfolded his arms, leaned forward and asked, "Why haven't we been shown this in Scripture before? All we have ever heard is that we had better shape up and live by the law, or God will get us!"

"Do you mean even my quiet times and my *trying to do* what Jesus would do *could* actually defeat me and can be religious law?" Mattie quizzed.

"Yes, Mattie, it might," I replied. "It depends on your motive. When we struggle to live by 'six steps to this and four principles to that,' we make laws out of those principles. *We have often been told that principles make the Christian life work, but it is the life of Christ within us that makes the principles work!*"

"Well, you will have to explain how living out of the life of Christ happens, because I surely do not know," Darryl interjected.

"Don't worry, you are about to see how to live out of your union with Christ and His grace in your relationship with Mattie. For now, here are some Scriptures on law versus grace, which might be helpful to you two," I answered.

Romans 6:14 puts it this way, "For sin shall not be master over you, for you are not under law, but under grace." It is because "the power of sin *is* the law" (1 Corinthians 15:56; emphasis mine). The sin principle gets its strength and power from laws. Romans 7:8 says, "...for apart from the Law sin is dead." The truth is that sin has no power over us as born again believers, because we are no longer under the law but under grace. However, our living by our own efforts to comply with religious laws or our personal rules and demands will lead to sin and defeat in our lives.

There are two main points here:

1. A promise: "Sin shall not be master over you"
2. An *explanation* of the promise: "for you are not under the law, but under grace."

We are not under law:

Functions of law:

1. The law *exposes* sin (Romans 7:5–2; Romans 3:20; Galatians 3:24–25).
2. The law *excites* more sin (Romans 7:5; 8; 1 Corinthians 15:56).
3. The law *exasperates* us when we try to live by it (Romans 7:13–25).

We are under Grace:

Effects of Grace:

1. Grace *forgives* sin (Romans 8:1).
2. Grace *frees* from the power of sin (Romans 8:2–4; 6:6–7).
3. Grace *fulfills* the requirements of the law (Romans 8:4; Galatians 5:22–23).
4. Grace *fills* us with the Holy Spirit so that we can put to death the deeds of the body (Romans 8:6, 12, 13).

When we live out of our wrong beliefs (myths) about how we are to find acceptance, worth, fulfillment, contentment, security and a sense of connectedness, we *live under our own laws and rules and it has the same effect as trying to live under religious law!* It brings forth sin, which results in death (emotional separation) in our relationships. We understand from Scripture that the demands of the laws we put on ourselves and each other bring forth guilt, anger and frustration.

If we are struggling internally and trying hard, we are living by law rather than grace. We can often mix our personal rules with religious law and the consequence is that we find ourselves without peace or joy. We then become T.I.R.E.D.—feeling Trapped, Indicted, Responsible, Exposed and Defensive.

Following is a copy of the table, "Myths vs Truth," which I gave Darryl and Mattie and the other couples I counsel. You will find some of your own personal and religious laws listed here. **Highlight the beliefs that are similar to your own and the truth that counteracts them.**

MYTHS *vs.* TRUTH
(Needs are in bold)

Myths	Truth
1. I must control circumstances for me (and my family) to **be secure.**	1. I am secure because I am hidden with Christ in God (Colossians 3:3). All my needs are supplied in Christ. (Philippians 4:19). It is not by my power or strength, but by His Spirit (Zechariah 4:6). He is a shield to those who walk uprightly (Proverbs 2:7b, 11).
2. I must perform perfectly and avoid mistakes to be **accepted and acceptable** to God.	2. I am perfect in Christ; one Spirit with Him (Hebrews 10:14; 1 Corinthians 6:17). I have been made accepted by Him (Ephesians 1:6). Christ died that I would be the righteousness of God in Him (2 Corinthians 5:21)
3. I am responsible for my spouse's or another's emotional well-being. I must apologize if he or she isn't okay or if they do something wrong (or) I am accountable to God for my spouse.	3. Each one shall give account of himself to God (Romans 14:12). I cannot rescue my brother by any means (Psalm 49:7). Each person eats the fruit of his *own* way (Proverbs 1:31).
4. I must stay emotionally guarded to be **safe and secure.**	4. The Lord is my safety (Psalm 4:8; 27:1-6; 32:7-11). Safety is only of the Lord (Proverbs 1:33; 3:23; 21:31). As I trust Christ, His peace will guard my heart and mind (Philippians 4:7). He is my shield and fortress (Psalm 18:1-3).
5. I must be strong and independent **to survive.**	5. Christ's strength is perfect in my weakness (2 Corinthians 12:9). My life is to be dependent on Christ, since He is the Vine and I am a branch in Him. Without Him I can do *nothing* (John 15:5; 2 Corinthians 12:10).

Myths	Truth
6. I do not measure up. I am not worthy of love. I may deserve to be punished.	6. Christ has made me accepted in Him (Ephesians 1:6; Psalm 139:13-18). I am chosen, have been made righteous, holy, a saint. I have been justified. I have been made a new creation (2 Corinthians 5:17; 1 Peter 2:9; 1 Corinthians 1:2; Romans 8:30).
7. Real men do not show they need help.	7. When I humble myself before God, in due time He exalts me (1 Peter 5:6). Pride comes before a fall (Proverbs 16:18).
8. I must improve myself and build my self-confidence to succeed and know I am **valued**.	8. My confidence is to be in the Lord, not myself (Proverbs 3:26; 14:26; I am to put no confidence in my flesh (Philippians 3:3). I am to humble myself and become of no reputation (Philippians 2:5-8).
9. I must get respect from my mate and others to know I am **of worth**.	9. I am called to love and to serve others and consider them better than myself (Philippians 2:3). Pride comes before destruction and shame (Proverbs 16:18; 11:2). I am to become of "no reputation" and be a servant (Philippians 2:5-8). He has made me accepted and perfect (Ephesians 1:6; Hebrews 10:14).
10. I must be heard and/or right to know I am **of value** to my loved one or others.	10. I am not to be wise in my own eyes (Proverbs 3:7). I am to find my value in Christ (Ephesians 1:6; See #9).
11. I must "fix and direct" if things are to go right for me and if I am going to be **secure and at peace**. (I must control interactions and circumstances.)	11. God will work all things together for good for me if I love Him and am called according to His purpose (Romans 8:28). He is faithful and will cause it to happen (1 Thessalonians 5:24). God works His will in the army of heaven and among the inhabitants of the earth (Daniel 4:35; God will accomplish that which concerns me (Psalm 138:8).

Myths	Truth
12. I must be the best to find **worth and security**.	12. The least shall be the greatest (Luke 9:48). God is my worth, security, my shield and Fortress (See #17; Proverbs 2:7b). Safety is of the Lord (Proverbs 21:31; Jeremiah 16:19).
13. Emotions represent truth.	13. Jesus Christ said He is the Truth. Emotions do not represent truth and are not to be trusted (John 14:6).
14. My **peace** is tied to my spouse's and/or others' opinions and to my being treated fairly. To **be fulfilled**, I am entitled to my spouse treating me the way the Lord commands him/her to.	14. Jesus Christ is my peace and gives me peace (John 14:2). I am in perfect peace as my mind is fixed on Him. As I humble myself, I will enjoy peace (Psalm 37:11; Isaiah 26:3 See # 32, 37).
15. Husbands and wives should **complete** each other.	15. Each has been made complete in Christ (Colossians 2:10).
16. Others and losses are responsible for my pain. My emotional **peace**, or lack of it, is somebody else's fault (or responsibility).	16. I am responsible to receive and walk in the healing, recovery, comfort, peace and restoration from Christ (Isaiah 61:1a-3; 58:8a; 54:1-14; Psalm 23:3).
17. I must prove I am right to know I am **of worth**.	17. Christ has made me accepted in Him (Ephesians 1:6; # 9, #10 Psalm 139:13-18). I am chosen, righteous, holy, a saint: A new creation (2 Corinthians 5:17; 1 Peter 2:9; 1 Corinthians 1:2).
18. I can't help being depressed and without hope if my circumstances don't change.	18. Christ gives me hope and a garment of praise for a spirit of heaviness (Romans 15:13; Psalm 16:11, 27:14, 31:24; Isaiah 61:3). Hope is not based on circumstances, but is only in Christ (1 Timothy 1:1; Colossians 1:27; Romans 15:13).

Myths	Truth
19. I must explain, justify and defend myself. I must please my spouse and/or others to avoid rejection and find **acceptance**.	19. Christ is my defender and my justifier (Romans 5:1; Colossians 3:3; Isaiah 54:17; Psalm 91:11; Acts 13:39). God will make my enemies to be at peace with me when my way pleases Him (Proverbs 16:7).
20. I must live under the burden of guilt if another isn't okay or if I have failed or sinned.	20. There is no condemnation to me as I walk after the Spirit. Christ came to make me perfect in my conscience (John 3:18; Romans 8:1; Hebrews 9:9, 14). I am forgiven of all my sins (Colossians 2:13).
21. I can't **be okay** unless I can trust my loved one.	21. I must put no confidence in human flesh (Philippians 3:3).
22. What I do makes me who I am.	22. Birth determines my identity. I have been made a new creation by my new birth. The old me died with Christ (Galatians 2:20; 2 Corinthians 5:17).
23. I must live in shame from abuse in my early years. It affects my life and I can't get over it.	23. As I trust Christ, I will forget the shame of my youth. Instead of shame, He will give me double honor. He came to heal my broken heart and give beauty for ashes. He will restore the years the locusts have eaten. My recovery will spring forth quickly (Isaiah 58:8a; Isaiah 61:1a,3,7; 54:4-8). Jesus said we have sorrow, but he gives us truth which brings healing and freedom (John 16:6,7)
24. My **emotional security** is based on my maintaining my structure and on connectedness with my spouse and/or my significant others.	24. Christ is my strong tower, etc. I am complete in Him (Colossians 2:10). He will establish, strengthen and settle me (1 Peter 5:10). He is my shield (Psalm 18:1-3).

Myths	Truth
25. I am inadequate.	25. I have been made adequate (2 Corinthians 3:5-6). I can do all things through Christ. I am complete in Him (Colossians 2:10; Philippians 4:13). He makes me adequate to do His will (Hebrews 13:21; See # 34).
26. I can't have any **peace or contentment** if my loved one doesn't change.	26. Christ is my peace. He gives me peace (John 14:27). When I cease from my own way, I have rest (Hebrews 4:10). Peace is mine through Christ (John 14:27). When I humble myself, I will delight in an abundance of peace (Psalm 37:11).
27. I can't help being anxious when the future is uncertain.	27. As I humble myself and cast my fears on God, He will exalt me in due time (1 Peter 5:6,7). I am to be anxious for nothing (Philippians 4:6). God will preserve and sustain me as I trust Him (Psalm 16:8a, 9, 11b; Psalm 23:4). The Lord preserves those who love Him (Psalm 3:23; 145:2; Proverbs 2:8). I am not to be afraid, for I dwell in the shelter of the Most High God (Psalm 91:1,5,6,10; Psalm 18:1-3). I am not to be troubled nor fearful (John 14:27).
28. I cannot be happy if I do not get my needs of **worth and security** met by my spouse or another.	28. See all of the above. He shall supply ALL my needs according to His riches in glory by Christ Jesus (Philippians 4:19).
29. If I am treated unfairly, it makes me a doormat.	29. Even though trials and unfairness will come to all, the Lord has made me who I am (# 31; # 2). Those reviling my good behavior shall be put to shame (1 Peter 3:17). As I walk in righteousness, no weapon formed against me shall prosper (Isaiah 54:17).

Myths	Truth
30. The Lord has never cared enough about me to answer my prayers.	30. If I abide in Him, I can ask and it will be given (John 15:7). If I ask and don't receive in God's timing, I have asked with the wrong motive (James 4:2,3; 1 John 3:22; 5:14).
31. If the Lord wanted good things for me, He wouldn't have allowed so much loss and pain.	31. Tribulation and trials will come to all, beginning with God's people. But Christ has overcome these things on my behalf (1 Peter 1:6; 4:12, John 16:33). He has plans for my good and desires to satisfy me with good things (Jeremiah 29:11; Psalm 103:5a). After I have experienced a trial, trusting Him, He will establish, strengthen and perfect me (1 Peter 5:10).
32. If the Lord cared about me, He would give me a person to fill my loneliness—make me **complete and fulfilled**. I need a person to complete me.	32. I will remain lonely unless I die to my own way of trying to make things work for me (John 12:24). He wants to fill me and my loneliness with Himself. I am to find my completeness in Christ. (Colossians 3:3, Ephesians 5:17,18).
33. I must see that others pay for the wrongs they have done against me.	33. God will avenge, vindicate me. I must release others from what they owe so that I won't suffer tormenting emotions (Romans 12:19; Hebrews 10:30,31; Matt. 18:23-35).
34. I don't have the power to love and serve.	34. When I cease my own trying and trust Him, Christ is faithful and He will do it. He gives me the victory. It is not by my power, nor strength, but by His Spirit that I accomplish (1 Thessalonians 5:24; 1 Corinthians 15:57; Zechariah 4:6). I can do all things through Christ who is my strength. The Lord will accomplish that which concerns Me (Psalm 138:8; Philippians 4:13).

Myths	Truth
35. My **worth and value** should come from hard work and responsibility.	35. My value and worth are only found in who Christ has made me—not in my performance. Christ has made me accepted in Him (Ephesians 1:6; Psalm139:13-18). My confidence is to be in the Lord, not myself (Proverbs 3:26; 14:26) I am to put no confidence in my flesh (Philippians 3:3).
36. My **security and value** should come from my loved one protecting and providing for me *or* doing certain things for me.	36. The Lord in me is my provider, my security, my worth. He preserves me as I walk in faith (Psalm 31:23; 145:20; 97:10; Proverbs 2:8; Also see # 17, #4).
37. I should find **significance** from another's love, appreciation and acceptance. I must have everyone's love and approval to feel good about myself and be **emotionally okay.**	37. See #35. I am not entitled to others meeting my needs. My needs are to be met in Christ. I am complete in Him. He will fill me (Philippians 4:19; Colossians 2:10; Ephesians 5:17,18).
38. **Satisfaction and fulfillment** should come from my marital partner.	38. The Lord will satisfy my hungry soul as I walk in His (Isaiah 58:10). He will fill me with His Spirit (Ephesians 5:17,18).
39. I am not **blessed** if God doesn't give me the things I want, according to my reason and timing. Things must go my way for me to be happy and satisfied.	39. God's ways are higher than my ways. He is in control and works all things together for my good if I love Him and am called according to His purpose. As I trust God and do not lean on my own understanding, He will direct my paths (Proverbs 3:5; Romans 8:28). He has plans for my good, to give me hope and a future (Jeremiah 29:11). Only He knows the times and seasons under His authority.
40. I must earn any good thing to enjoy from God.	40. He has freely given me all things to enjoy. I am justified freely by His grace (Romans 3:24; 1 Corinthians 2:12; 1 Timothy 6:17; Matthew 10:8).

Myths	Truth
41. I must have everyone's love and approval to feel good about myself and be **okay emotionally.**	41. See # 35, 37, 38. I can't count on others approval for meeting my needs of worth, validation and significance. These needs are met in Christ.
42. I must struggle to surrender or put away the flesh (my old "survival strategies").	42. I must not try to put them away. If my mind is set on the Spirit, I will enjoy life and peace. When I just cease from my *own* works, then I will have rest and peace. When I abide in Christ, I will I have joy (John 15:11; Hebrews 4:10). As I walk after the Spirit, (abiding and focusing on the Spirit), I won't fulfill the desires of the flesh (Galatians 5:16).
43. Life must be fair for me to be **calm.** I am a victim and cannot be okay until I am no longer victimized.	43. Life is not fair. Trials and injustices will come to all. I enter into Christ's victory as I take up my trial (cross) daily and deny myself. I *cannot* follow Christ unless I do this. Calmness and peace are found only in Christ (See # 31, #14, Matthew 16:24, 14:33.)
44. My childhood issues must be dealt with before I can be okay.	44. My issues *have* been dealt with because I have died with Christ and am a new creation. I am okay when I recognize that He has given me the Victory and cease from my struggling (See # 34, #22, Hebrews 4:10.)
45. If I *punish* my spouse or others, then they will love me and give me what I need.	45. I will eat the fruit of my *own* way. I will reap what *I* sow. If I sow to the flesh, I will reap corruption! As I am unselfish and love my spouse and others (sow to the Spirit), I will reap that eternal life of Christ's sufficiency for me (Matthew 5:46; Galatians 6:7, 8; Proverbs 1:31).

Myths	Truth
46. Love must be earned. I must please God and/or others to be **loved and accepted**. I must know I am loved by and important to another to be okay.	46. God loved me when I was a sinner. He freely gives me all things to enjoy. He has made me accepted in Him. I do not have to have acceptance from a person for my needs to be met. Love is my *sacrifice* of my old survival strategies; it is not "getting." ALL my needs are met in Christ (See #40, #2, John 15:13; Philippians 4:19.)
47. I should not have adversity or opposition in life, relationships or marriage.	47. See # 29, #31. I know that trials come to all, and I should not be surprised when they come. God allows them to happen so that I won't depend on myself but on God (2. Corinthians 1:9).
48. Others are to blame (are responsible) for how I feel. It is someone's fault. I am a victim.	48. I am responsible for me (See # 3.) He came to restore and heal my broken soul (Luke 4:18. See also # 16, 18, 26, 45).
49. Things must go my way for me to be fulfilled or satisfied.	49. See # 37, 38, 39. Fulfillment only comes from the Lord. He will fill me with His Spirit. He will Satisfy my hungry soul and quench my thirst (John 4:14).

Chapter 11

Disarming Hijackers: Confronting Myths

On the Map: Couples, still in the wilderness, continue to hold on to weapons that are old familiar myths, beguiling anticipations. They go around the same mountain again and again, not learning...

Myths hijack marital relationships as couples travel on their journeys. *Couples resist changing myths (old beliefs) because they do not know that wrong thinking is the culprit behind defeating behaviors and damaging emotions. Thinking must be changed* if our couples want to turn from their wilderness wandering and go out to experience God's best. The word *repentance* means to turn around and go in a different direction by *a change of mind, thinking, or attitude.*

In this chapter, we will confront and disarm a few commonly held myths about marriage. Among them are: "We are entitled," "We become one person at the marriage union," "We must get attuned to each other for the marriage to be right," "We are wired to find satisfaction in our work and accomplishments," "If we don't communicate our feelings, we cannot have intimacy" and "It is passivity to depend on Christ to be our fulfillment and to live His life through us." Other myths will be addressed as we progress through the book.

Entitled: Katrina

When I assigned the handout, "Myths of Marriage," for homework, Tony and Katrina returned to their counseling session with differing responses. Tony had a few questions, but Katrina took strong exception, saying it was an extremist view. She stared at her lap, crossed her long arms and legs and jiggled her foot.

She said, "This list says that he doesn't have to do things to help around the house and I should do it all. It says that he doesn't have to listen to me and respect my opinions. It is also saying he doesn't have to act in his role as head of the home!" When I asked Katrina to explain how she got *that* from the list, she replied, "Well, even if those things were not actually said, they were implied. I believe I am entitled to those things!"

It took a little time to show Katrina that just because one is not *entitled* to certain things, it doesn't mean that the mate is not to do what the Lord commands. It is just that one has no *entitlements* to what the other should do and no right to demand those things from the other. *There are no scriptural promises to spouses that the other one will do what God commands!* Suddenly, they understood.

Becoming one person: Tony

Tony confronted the last myth on the sheet I had given them. It was, "We become one person at the marriage union." He quizzed, "But I have always heard that we become one when we marry. Doesn't that mean we should think alike, have the same desires and interests, intuitively know the other's desires and so on? Shouldn't there be some 'rights' attached to that?"

I answered that this kind of closeness would be like a fusion with each other and would obscure individuality and our unique personalities. It would lead to emotional dependency, which is a barrier to intimacy. True intimacy is different. It requires accepting differences, the spouse's limitations and one's losses. It involves dealing with conflicts. It means knowing who we are in Christ as individuals.

When Scripture speaks of becoming one, it is referring to the physical, sexual union. There is much misunderstanding of the Scriptures that speak of husbands and wives "being one flesh." Many people have expressed the belief that these verses mean husbands and wives become *one person*—and should live like it! This means they should like the same things, agree on all points, intuitively know what the other is thinking, do everything together and live as extensions of each other. Nothing could be further from the truth! Scriptures that refer to "being one flesh" are: Matthew 19:5,6; Mark 10:8; 1 Corinthians 6:16; Ephesians 5:31.

Ephesians 5:32 speaks of marriage being "a great mystery...concerning Christ and the church" and of our being members of His body. Ephesians 5:31 says, "For this reason a man shall leave his father and mother and be joined to his wife, and the two shall become one flesh" (NKJV). In these verses as well as the other references, the Greek word for *flesh* is *sarx,* which means the "physical body." So where the Scripture speaks of two being "one flesh," it is referring to the *sexual union*. The sexual union of husbands and wives is a mystery in that it is symbolic of believers being united with Christ—being one Spirit with Him.

From the day that I addressed these "Myths of Marriage" for Tony and Katrina, their counseling began to slowly turn around. Although they continued to struggle, they truly wanted to understand what happened to them when they became new creations and how to live out the truths of grace and freedom in Christ within the marriage. *I explained that the Christian life must be lived out in relationships of some kind, that an individual cannot live on a deserted island and live out the Christian life!*

Ephesians 5: 31—"The two shall become one"

In these Scriptures,
Matthew 19:5,6; Mark 10:8; 1 Corinthians 6:16;
the phrase "be one flesh"

refers to the sexual union.

Flesh = *sarx* (Greek) = Physical body

✝

The husband's and wife's sexual union is symbolic of Christ's union with believers who are referred to as the Church.

✝

To "be one" in these Scriptures DOES NOT refer to two individuals *being blended into one person,* where each completes the other, has the same desires, wills, thoughts and opinions as the other!

Marriage DOES unite two individuals *who are to remain two individuals, each being complete in Christ.*

Attuned to each other: Darryl and Mattie

Darryl said, "What we are learning is great, but when we first came to counseling, we wanted you to teach us some marriage skills so we could become more attuned to each other. We were under the impression that's what marriage is all about."

I said that I didn't want to try to get them attuned to each other. They asked me to explain. I gave them the piano illustration. "Imagine if I were a piano tuner. A man brings two out-of-tune pianos to me and tells me he wants them attuned to each other. The goal is to have them as perfectly matched in quality of tone as possible. How do you think this could be done?" They scratched their heads. I said, "It won't happen by trying to get them attuned to each other, because each is out of tune."

The light came on and Mattie responded, "You would have to tune each one to the same tuning fork." "Exactly," I replied. "When each marital partner is intimately attuned to Christ, trusting and abiding in Him, then each *will be* intimately attuned to the other!"

The Pianos

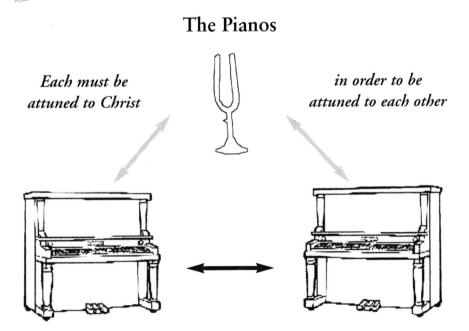

Each must be attuned to Christ

in order to be attuned to each other

As couples begin to understand the truth, I often use the piano illustration to help show them what being separate in Christ means. *The spouses must be free and separate in Christ before they can walk in unity with the other.* They learn to be separate in Christ as they depend on Him to fulfill emotional needs, be their protection, their completer and to live His life out through them. Trusting Christ in this way means they must surrender reliance on old myths and strategies. Walking "in agreement" with Scripture means each walking in the truth. It doesn't mean having the same opinions, desires and thoughts as each other!

"But we are wired...": John and Diane

A former client of mine, John, was serious and rigid while his wife, Diane, was naturally beautiful and carefree. Diane expected John to validate and fulfill her by giving her time and attention. John was a workaholic and looked to his job and to orderliness to find satisfaction. He felt responsible to see to it that Diane kept his kind of order at home, which was difficult since organization was not her gift. Although he loved Diane very much, he was fatigued and felt he had nothing to give when Diane pursued him. He put her down for being *too* carefree and spontaneous. He was fighting feelings of anger and resentment.

Their myths had been identified in counseling and the couple had been presented with the contrasting truths of Christ's provision for them. I illustrated how dependence was to be on Christ as the Source for meeting one's needs of Contentment, Security and Worth rather than one's mate or job.

John was resistant. He countered with, "But we both believe we have been 'wired' to find satisfaction from our work and accomplishments. We have been 'wired' to gain respect and satisfaction from our mate's responses to us!" These beliefs are some of those *beguiling anticipations* that have been around since the beginning. The harder John and Diane tried to get satisfaction from work and each other, the more T.I.R.E.D. they became.

I pointed out that if we are operating independently of our Source, there is no lasting satisfaction in anything we do. Dan Stone and Doug

Smith, in their book, *The Rest of the Gospel*, identify "walking after flesh" as, "the soul operating independently of its Source" (p. 100). *If we cease struggling and depend on Christ to accomplish our work through us and meet our needs, then we will find fulfillment in whatever we do.*

Adam found satisfaction in his work in the Garden before the fall when he was still operating from his Source, God. It was after his disobedience to God that work was no longer fulfilling, because Adam had become his own source of trying to find contentment. *It was at that time of his disobedience and his separation from God that he became "wired" to try to fill the neediness by his or another's (Eve's) performance.*

John and Diane knew they had new natures in Christ. However, they needed to realize that the "wiring" or neediness they felt in their soul was inherited from Adam and Eve. They needed to understand the truth that Jesus Christ came to restore their souls and satisfy their neediness.

John was endeavoring to justify his theological position. Yet, he had never realized the fulfillment he hoped for, in spite of some extraordinary achievements. I urged John and Diane to "risk" believing God and to let go of their inner struggle to make life work for them (See Psalm 46.)

"If we do not communicate about our hurt feelings, we can't have intimacy": Mattie

"I have tried all of our married life to get Darryl to share his feelings and to listen to mine. We just can't have intimacy if we don't communicate our hurt feelings to each other," Mattie lamented.

I had to explain to Mattie that good communication in marriage is necessary. But *one's trying to get the other to talk about hurt or damaging emotions is an effort to get one's own hurting or angry emotions validated!* That is, we want our mate to understand how hurt we are so he/she will change to make us okay. This says that our mate is responsible for our emotional well-being, which is a false belief. *If damaging emotions are validated, we also validate the myths that cause those emotions.* I will explain about not living out of emotions later in the book.

"That is passivity...": John

John reasoned again, "This sounds like passivity you're talking about when you refer to Christ accomplishing our work, being our protection, our defender to others and so on. And I don't buy it." He added, "We know that doing our work involves struggling. Sometimes it is extremely hard."

Acknowledging that it could sound like passivity, I pointed out that trusting the Lord to do these things in and through us is not outwardly doing nothing. Rather, it is ceasing from the *internal* struggle to have it our way and from operating by our old myths. Diane responded with, "Oh, you are talking about a change in our *attitudes*."

I replied, "Thank you!"

In *The Sacred Romance*, Curtis and Eldridge tell us,

We anesthetize our hearts from feeling their emptiness by competence or order of some kind, with redemptive busyness, or by some form of indulgence. And to free ourselves by will power or external discipline is futile. The only power is in the attitude of our internal being—the choice of our heart (p. 154).

We learned early in our lives to involve ourselves in the strategies of which Curtis and Eldridge spoke. So we struggle, we fear, we become depressed, we become lonely and depleted. We believe that the way to freedom and fulfillment is by *external* "doing," which is prompted by what seems right to us. But any "doing" of value must be an *internal* choice of the heart to rely on Christ and any external action that follows is *Christ's doing*!

God's intention is that He live His life out through us. This means that we choose to be the conduit through which He will live. I illustrated to John that *our struggle to keep walking after our old ways prevents us from experiencing Christ's living His life out through us.* It hinders us from drinking of the river that would flow out! It blocks us from experiencing the contentment, the sense of being "right" before God and the joy the Lord wants us to know in our work and relationships. When we struggle to make things work for us, we frustrate God's grace that He freely gives us.

John, as many husbands and wives, wrestled with the idea of surrendering his overly-responsible ways. Latoya, the strong independent client with the coffee and cream complexion, was also confused by this. Their strategies resulted from believing that one must struggle in life to hold things together in order to keep themselves and their families secure and meet material needs. But anxiety always follows. It is foreign to begin believing and living from the truth that Jesus spoke in Matthew 6:31–33 when He said for us *not to be anxious* about providing these things, but if we would seek first His kingdom and His righteousness, all these things would be added to us. Remember, this is not passivity. Later we will see what it means to seek Christ's kingdom and righteousness.

Although Diane was beginning to catch on, John was still striving to live in both the natural world of his baggage and the supernatural world of faith. And it can't be done. This is what Scripture refers to as being *double-minded*. John 1:8 says that a double-minded person won't receive from God.

John and Diane had wandered in circles in a dry wasteland as all the others I have mentioned. Soon their journey, as well as the journeys of all the couples, would bring them to a place where they would have an opportunity to have relief from their hurts and disappointments.

Just intellectually knowing the truths we have discussed would not bring them the freedom and satisfaction they longed for, but it was a necessary beginning.

The couples are about to discover the way out of the wilderness! Their paths have led to a river, and crossing it will be the only way out of that desert of fatigue and disillusionment. At the same time, it will be the only way into experiencing God's faithfulness and the reality of His promises. One must choose to cross alone, and there is no assurance one's mate will also make the same decision or that he or she will go across at the same time.

"We must have the same opinions to have intimacy": Katrina

Katrina spoke from her emotional dependency when she said, "We rarely have the same opinions about anything from the way to wash dishes to political views to the way we deal with our families. Doesn't the Bible say that we should be in agreement?"

I replied, "In Philippians 1:27, Paul expresses his desire that the church body stand firm in one Spirit with one mind. This does not mean all should have the same opinions. It is not expected that two mates have the same views and opinions on matters to have intimacy. Paul says this in the context of striving together for the faith of the gospel. It is in trusting the Lord that all believers should be of one mind—one goal. This is similar to the example of each being "attuned" to the Lord. But this is not something that one person is entitled to from the other. This will be more evident as we progress through the book.

"I must see to it that my spouse does what is right": Tony

Tony struggled with Katrina being rude to his family. He would sulk for days when she wasn't respectful to them. I explained again that *even if he is right*, it is not his job to try to make her do what God commands or to punish her if she doesn't do the right thing. There has been a teaching among Christians that the husband is accountable to God for the spouse. However, Romans 14:12 tells us that each one of us shall give account of himself to God.

Part Three

THE REST OF THE JOURNEY: UNFAMILIAR TERRITORY

Chapter 12

A River to Cross: A Choice to Make

On the Map: Crossing Jordan into Canaan. Jordan is a picture of the cross and death to the old ways.

The travelers were exhausted and needed relief from their wandering in the desert—the wilderness. They were T.I.R.E.D.—feeling Trapped, Indicted, Responsible, Exposed and Defensive. In Deuteronomy 1:6–8, it records that God told the Israelites they had stayed in the desert long enough. He told them to turn and set their journey and go. God said, "See, I have placed the land before you; go in and possess the land...." He was referring to the land of Canaan that He had promised His people.

The couples desperately needed to drink of the Water of life that would quench their thirst. They needed rest and the abundant life—their inheritance in Christ—to experience within their marriages. But all of this lay in the land on the other side of the Jordan River. The road had led them to the banks of a stormy river at flood stage, and they were left wondering how to get across because there were neither boats nor bridges for them to take.

The things they needed and longed for were to be possessed beyond the river, and there was one way to get to the other side. They had arrived at the place on the journey where they had to make some choices if they were to leave the wilderness. They had to be willing to leave, or surrender, reliance on old possessions, expectations, self-preservations and other baggage. They had to be ready to choose to spend intimate time with God as they focused on truth in order to move forward in faith. And they had to believe that the Lord would see that they got across. They had never exercised this kind of faith before.

Some had heard reports from a few who had been across that the promises of God's abundance over there were indeed true, but there were obstacles over on the other side. They had heard that some of the inhabitants there had waged war against the ones who had already crossed. So they were reluctant. It was unfamiliar territory and it sounded scary. They recalled how the Lord had parted the Red Sea and brought them out of their Egyptian captivity. But the Jordan River wasn't opening the same way. Then someone remembered the Lord had told Israel that *He* brought them out of their captivity so that *they* might go in and possess the land that belonged to them. So it was *their choice*. Others had heard reports of Jordan beginning to part, one step at a time, for people who relinquished their baggage and just *stepped out in faith*. Self-effort wouldn't take them across. Willpower would be useless.

What a choice! The couples were standing on the banks of Jordan considering the price of crossing. They had been told that Canaan, on the other side, was the only place they would find what they longed for in life and marriage. I related to them the story of a rich young prince who chose not to leave dependency on his possessions at this point on the journey and consequently went away sorrowful (Matthew 19:16–29). He loved his possessions more. He never experienced that abundance and freedom that lay across the river.

My Dad had always referred to *physical* death as "crossing the River Jordan." So, in his best tenor, Harold Smith sang a type of eulogy, "I Won't Have to Cross Jordan Alone," as we all stared at the closed casket at the front of the country church. My chest tightened as I dealt with the various thoughts and emotions surrounding my own sense of connectedness the loss of a parent brings.

We try hard to find a sense of belonging in our human relationships, and we even have a certain security and familiarity with our old ways.

When a person is faced with relinquishing those old familiar loves that often anesthetize the heart, it feels almost like the loss of death. In fact, crossing Jordan *means* death—our *dying to* reliance on our old ways, to our living independently from God. Setting up housekeeping on the other side of the river in the new and unfamiliar land of Canaan will mean repeating many times our death *to* the strategies by which we attempted to find life, fill our emptiness and drive away our loneliness.

The River: Tony and Katrina

Tony wore his usual red shirt with the company logo and Katrina fingered her familiar hoop earrings. Both were uneasy in the counseling session and I learned it was because they were not ready to face the river yet. The prospect was threatening and scary. Even after learning something about their new identity and possessions in Christ, Tony, who was usually laid back, had shouted, "But why? Why does it have to be this way? If God is good and wants us to experience good things, why would He allow so many years of being misunderstood—so much pain?" I replied that I would soon address his question.

Katrina's foot jiggled as she stared in her lap. She was angry, "Where was God when I was abused if He is a good God and wants the best for us?" She had concluded in childhood that there is no safety in life, because neither God nor people can be trusted. Katrina still saw herself as a victim and most people as victimizers. She wasn't ready to trust God and step into the river.

Curtis and Eldridge, in the *Sacred Romance*, say,

> There is no escaping your identity. You will not live beyond how you see yourself; not for long. If Failure is the part you're playing, you will fail. The Performers will perform, the Seductive will seduce, the Victims will be victimized, the Nobodies will fade away, and the Somebodies will do whatever it is that makes them feel like somebody (p. 89).

We, as Katrina, defeat ourselves by listening to echoes from the past—beliefs about ourselves and Satan's using these things to cleverly deceive us after we have been made new creations. We are angry at ourselves and others who have "caused" us pain.

The River: Latoya

Since Latoya had been in the same counseling process as the couples, she had also come to the river and was struggling over the idea of surrendering old familiar ways. I quoted Greg Smith when he spoke to our lay counselors,

> When God allows the plight we are in, we think He is working against us. Well, in a way He is. He desires to use it to frustrate our self-redemptive ways; our survival strategies and defense mechanisms that we utilize to preserve ourselves.

God does this to drive us to the end of our focus being on us and the injustices in our relationships to the beginning of our mind being set on Him as our Source. In other words, He allows us to see that our fleshly ways aren't working, to discourage us from walking after the flesh! He wants us to see that we can't get from another or by our performance what only He gives. It is then that we are willing to allow change to come. We must *cease* our *struggle* to find fulfillment or even material security by our own ways.

Latoya's human reason still told her that she and the family would suffer severe lack if she didn't struggle to try to maintain control over the finances. But eventually she made the decision from her heart to surrender her control to God and believe His promises that He would supply their needs. I had explained this does not mean passivity.

I often quote a familiar little saying to my couples at this point. It is, "If you do what you've always done, you will get what you always got!" *In other words, without surrendering reliance on myths of self-effort, self-advancement, self-protection, self-sufficiency and entitlements* (which lead to behaviors that can look good *or* bad), *we cannot expect anything to be different.* We, as the Israelites, will just continue to go around the same mountain again and again experiencing the same disappointments, hurts, emptiness and fatigue as we live with our mate.

Individuals may be facing the river and still not understand what they must relinquish.

I will frequently use the word *surrender*, which means "to give up possession of or power over; to give up claim to; to yield or give over, especially as in favor of another; to yield or voluntarily resign one's self; to relinquish." And *to yield* means "to concede, to surrender under pressure." I will use both words interchangeably. In Romans 6 (KJV) we are told to yield ourselves to God and that we are to yield ourselves as servants, or slaves, unto righteousness. This is spoken of as *obedience*. This has the connotation of death to the flesh.

Sometimes I give the couples I counsel questions to ask themselves that are helpful in identifying anything more they might be holding on to that must be surrendered to God. Following is a copy of those questions. You may answer them for yourself. They were adapted from a set of questions developed by Mike Quarles.

Briefly Answer Each Question

*These questions may help you identify anything
that still remains to be surrendered.*

1. What is the long-standing goal that you can't seem to attain in your life and marriage? *Christian marriage + Christ centered kids*

2. If you could, what would you change about your spouse and present circumstances?

3. What is your greatest fear in life? How is this related to your spouse?

4. What strategies of trying to get your needs met and protect yourself would feel the most risky to let go of in your relationship with your mate?

5. What do you resist the most in your marital relationship?

6. Is there anything about your life, (appearance, character, relationships, status, past, your spouse, extended family, finances) that you cannot accept? What?

7. May God do anything He wants with you?

8. Which of your rules or myths do you still resist yielding?

The River: Darryl and Mattie

Graying Darryl in his crisply starched shirt and the proper English teacher Mattie answered the questions and identified additional things that had prevented their surrendering themselves to God. **I said that it is not just the "things" that must be surrendered or yielded to God—to the life of Christ within—but** *ourselves,* **which includes** *the things.* This means that our dependency on our myths—our controls, protections, pride, strategies and entitlements—must be relinquished.

Mattie revealed, "The questions helped me to see the thing I fear most is Darryl's withdrawing from me, withholding affection and not cherishing me or valuing my emotions. I have always felt I must have that connectedness and assurance to be an emotionally whole person. I *know* I must come to a place of allowing the Lord to fill that longing and protect my heart."

Darryl added, "I saw that what *I* fear most is Mattie's criticism, nagging and her reminding me of my responsibilities. And I hate it when she answers questions others direct at *me* and when she interrupts and talks over me. I need to let go of my presumed right to approval, to not be harshly accused and criticized. I thought I had a right to withdraw and protect myself from her criticisms. I have to learn to remember who I am in Christ and that what she says or does doesn't make me who I am." It was huge thing for them to confess these things from the heart.

He said, "You know, I believed I surrendered when I received Christ. But now I realize how much I had depended on my own strategies to satisfy my needs and to protect myself emotionally in my life and marriage. It has been hard for me to realize that these ways are living independently from God and are sin—especially if they look good. I have lived constantly with anger, because I felt my rights were violated. But now, I must trust that Christ indwells my spirit and is in a place where it is possible to experience His emotional protection. I know I don't have a right to my own protective space. I'm definitely not living in this truth yet, but I want to."

As Darryl and Mattie lived out of their old strategies of emotional pursuing and distancing, each was living out of the other's responses.

This held them hostage, and they longed to be free. They needed to relinquish their old ways.

I believe it is valuable to "do some business" with God and pray a prayer of surrender. This outward action of the attitude of the heart can be a landmark you can look back to and remind yourself that it happened. *We surrender our acting independently of God and to dependency on Him.* In Kay Ruff's words, "God takes surrender very seriously. It won't cost you anything... *it will cost you everything!*"

I clarified to them that surrender is not a one-time choice. It is a daily re-affirming the choice one has made. It isn't as if you walk through a door and there will be no more hard times. The living of the Christian life is a lifetime process, and it is okay if we fall down on the way. *And we will.*

"Head Knowledge" vs "Heart Knowledge"

Darryl and Mattie were facing the choice to trust God and surrender old thinking and old demands, not knowing what it meant for the future. As they faced the River Jordan with much contemplation, both remarked that they knew "in their heads" everything they had learned. Mattie revealed, "It is only head knowledge with me." Mattie, as many individuals, felt it had to become "heart knowledge" before she could step out, put her feet in the water and begin walking, because she didn't "feel it."

For something to become heart knowledge, we must act on what we know in our heads to be true concerning God's faithfulness, regardless of our emotions. I noted that with each step they take into the Jordan (surrendering in the face of a threatening situation), they will find God has upheld them and "parted the water." His faithfulness will become heart knowledge *as they go and arrive on the other side of the river (situation).* In the process, they will become "strengthened, established and settled" in their faith.

Praying a prayer of surrender simply involves a confession that the old strategies are the sins of self-sufficiency and living independently of God. It is also a resolve that from a certain point on, you desire to live a life of dependency on the Lord who indwells you. You must do this believing that Christ will meet your needs.

Our couple earnestly prayed the "Prayer of Surrender." They "faithed"! Faith isn't "conjuring up" a belief. It is making choices to trust God and go forth. Darryl and Mattie believed God and trusted Him to take them across. Darryl stepped out of his comfort zone and led the way. We will return to Mattie and Darryl's journey later.

Perhaps you are at a point where you would also like to make the choice to relinquish your old dependencies to God. You do not have to understand yet how it will all work. A sample "Prayer of Surrender" follows.

Prayer of Surrender: A Sample Prayer

By Don and Kay Ruff

Lord Jesus Christ,

In the process of my relinquishing control, a struggle ensues...because it is like falling off a cliff. There are rocks and boulders down there...I cling to everything that I think will sustain my life.

But I receive anything You wish to do with me, through me, to me...in my life, Lord, that would glorify You. I am willing to be content in any situation, because all my needs are met in Christ.

I will yield myself to you as you take me "over the cliff." I am probably going to resist, but I want you to persevere...I want you to bring me to the end of a walk where I depend on my own resources.

I surrender my own (fleshly) life to you and the Cross. I give up trusting my own way, and I relinquish my presumed rights to everything I thought I owned and was entitled to.

I believe Your Word when it says that I have been crucified with Christ, that sin no longer has any power over me and that I have been raised to walk in newness of life. Since I have been raised to sit in Heavenly places, I believe I am also seated on the right hand of the Father, in Christ. I believe You are in the Father and You indwell me. And I am in You, so we both are in the Father.

I trust that You are my very life now and You will do what I have never been able to do depending on myself. Teach me about who I am now that I am in Christ. If there is anything hindering your life from flowing out through me, please bring it to my attention.

I understand more clearly now how You are dealing with me...how Your desire is that Your life would be released into my outer man as you free me from reliance on myself. Deal with me in whatever particular way is needful for me to lay aside my presumed "rights" and "privileges." As you do this, convict me of my fleshly way and how destructive it is to me and my spouse. I love You, Lord.

I thank You and praise You. Manifest Yourself in my life.

Portions of the surrender prayer are adapted from concepts in Larry Crabb's book, *The Marriage Builder* and in Bill and Annabel Gillham's book, *He Said, She Said.*

The River: Tony and Katrina

Tony and Katrina continued to be caught up in emotional battles. Katrina stared at her lap and fingered an earring. She was wrestling with fear of relinquishing forever the emotional connectedness with Tony she wanted but which, at the same time, she feared and sabotaged. It was still too scary for her to trust God for her emotional safety and surrender her protective avoidance strategies.

In her first marriage, Katrina lived totally from her husband's opinions and responses to her to the point that she didn't know her own heart. She looked to him to validate her. Her emotions were based on his opinions of her. And when the marriage and her hopes of being affirmed by him failed, Katrina was so devastated that she decided not to open up to a mate again. Yet, as other people who see themselves as rejects, she leeched on to another person who seemed to accept her—Tony.

Tony was sulking and still bitter over his being shut out by Katrina. He wasn't ready to give up believing he was entitled to her making him feel of worth as a man. Neither was ready to make a choice to walk past what they felt and enter the river. Their emotions dominated everything they did. I was disappointed. But I had to remember that I couldn't change them.

The River: John and Diane

Eventually my former clients, rigid John and carefree Diane, came to the place of surrender. Diane was ready and surrender was a relief from feeling she should be responsible for John's emotions and responses. She also yielded her dependency on John to make her feel worthwhile and complete. It was unfamiliar territory to her and she felt uneasy. She had decided to make her choices based not on her emotions but on truth. This was tremendous growth.

John was a man of God and knew he must be willing to lose his old controls. Even though he still had unanswered questions, it was a release when he relinquished his presumed responsibility to give solutions to Diane, make her feel okay and see to it that she kept his kind of order at home. He also made the heart-choice to surrender having to gain acceptance by his influential position and by his accomplishments in ministry. He even told God that he yielded his struggle to control finances. All of this was uncomfortable and foreign to him.

John still expressed confusion about surrender as he asked, "If we relinquish all our old strategies by which we have identified ourselves, where do our unique personalities come in?" I helped him to see that our personalities are related to our own spiritual gift(s) being expressed through us as we walk after the Spirit.

Their surrender didn't mean they would never walk after old ways again. It meant they stepped out in faith with a resolve to always quickly return to an attitude of trust and death to the old controls as they moved through their life and marriage.

Neither understood *how* Christ would live out this life through them as they went, or how they would experience Him meeting their needs, but I assured them I would explain more as they stepped out in faith.

Chapter 13

Road Rage: Under Attack

> **On the Map: In Canaan.** It is a land flowing with milk and honey. But is a land where we may come under attack.

Darryl and Mattie: Road rage

I eagerly anticipated Darryl's and Mattie's upcoming counseling session. They had done some serious "business with God" when they yielded themselves, their myths and behaviors—their survival strategies—to the Lord the week before. Both had been convicted of the futility of their old ways, tears had flowed and both had left with fresh joy and hopefulness.

When they came in Mattie was solemn, and they sat on opposite ends of the sofa. Darryl crossed his legs and arms, facing away from Mattie and me. "Oh no," I thought, "What has happened?" I asked how they were doing. Silence.

"This isn't working," Darryl finally snipped.

They were quiet. I waited.

"*You* tell Anne what happened," he said, not moving his body from the fixed position.

"You tell her!" Mattie, the steel magnolia, was stilted. Her quirky shoulder moved forward as if to emphasize her words, "You are the one who lost control with your anger, yelled and withdrew from me and the kids again!"

Silence. Still fixed, Darryl turned only his head slightly to look at me. "Nothing has changed. She is still criticizing and demanding. A couple of days after we were in here, something happened that didn't suit her and she started telling me where I had failed the family and her. In fact, she told her sister on the phone and her sister sided with her. Nobody considers what *I* want!

"I can't take anymore. I was so hopeful last week. But I'm exhausted. I resent being the only one to surrender. Mattie won't tell you what else happened, but I will. We were at her sister's house and Mattie attacked me. She started on how I don't love or care about her. She was loud and made a scene. She said if I valued her I would change jobs and make more money so she wouldn't have so much responsibility."

Mattie was at the point of tears, "I just want you to help me more, listen to me and know what I want without my having to ask. If I have to ask for it, I wouldn't want it. It wouldn't mean anything."

Darryl responded, "No? But you'll sure punish me and not tell me why!"

The couple was experiencing what I call, "road rage." Temporarily reverting into an old familiar pattern is not unusual after individuals have come to a point of earnestly desiring submit to God and making an initial choice to surrender. I suspected that they needed to have a better comprehension of surrender and I wanted to encourage them.

I advised them that since all of us understood the root causes of their fighting and because they had chosen to humble themselves, relinquish old ways and focus on the truth as they spent some solitary time with the Lord, I was going to encourage them in that direction. I asked them to stick with the process, because I knew their yielding their hearts to the Lord had been real and they were close to experiencing victory. They agreed to my suggestions and to trust me at this point.

As Darryl's and Mattie's emotions calmed down to several notches less than "10," he admitted his confusion. "When we surrendered, I thought things would automatically be different since you told us the

Lord would live through us. I don't understand what happened. I know in my heart I surrendered to God and I've tried to stay yielded. Why can't we do it even for a week?"

"Darryl," I replied, "Do you remember when I told you that living this yielded life is a process, and you would fall down and blow it sometimes?"

"Yes."

I explained that a major point of surrender is that we choose it regardless of whether the other person does or not. I added that it was his *trying* to be yielded that was preventing his yieldedness!

Often folks in counseling will tell me they have surrendered many times, but they "keep taking it back." When I hear this, I relate the following illustration to help clarify the concept of surrender. "When I was a child, several of the sister churches in our community gathered for a picnic and swimming at Freeman's Lake. I recall Miss Rebecca, whose presence was quite balloon-like. While she wasn't aware of my staring at her, I was captured by the ease that a lady, whom I thought should sink, folded her arms behind her head and lay upon the water as if it were a bed. Miss Rebecca was *abiding* in the water, trusting that it would hold her up! *She had surrendered herself to it.* I was amazed at how she just rested there for long periods of time, because when I was learning to swim, *the harder I tried to float, the faster I sank!*

"My *trying* to surrender reliance on myself—my old strategies—is much like *trying* to float. The harder I try, the quicker I fail! That is because the emphasis is still on *me* and what *I can do.* **My focus must not be on the surrender.** I must continually *choose* to relax, *cease* my inner struggle to control my life, guard myself, get approval and find emotional security from my mate and others, while I focus on truths such as the ones listed on the 'Myths vs Truth' table and trust the life of Christ within me to fill and sustain me. I need to get intimate with the Father, thanking Him daily for these facts of grace. This is when I test the Lord's faithfulness to uphold me and meet my needs.

"Think about this," I reasoned. "We can't *try* to forget! If our focus is on trying to forget a thing, that thing is all we can think about. Surrender, being yielded to God, or denying self, whatever you want to call it, is like learning a new language. I will illustrate. Let's say that suddenly you are sent to Siberia. It is freezing, you need to know how to live in this new land and the language is unfamiliar. Nobody speaks English. You have been told you can't return home and you'll never hear English again. What do you think your *focus* is going to be on?"

Mattie responded, "Why, I guess it would be on trying to learning the language and understanding the ways of that new land."

"Exactly. *You will not be focused on trying to put away English,* but on *learning the new language.* Yielding ourselves to God as we cease from our own works is to be ongoing. It happens by our mind (and our heart) being set on fellowship with Him and living from truth and new attitudes rather than by our trying to stop old ways."

Scripture has various terms for the concept of surrender. But it really means to trust the Lord instead of ourselves, our own way, our own reason and strengths. It is a discipline—a choice—that must be made daily. In John 15, Jesus said He abides in us, and if we abide in Him, we can ask what we wish and it will be done. If we abide in Him, we *will be* asking within His will!

Since the mystery of Christ's life in us has been revealed, we are to no longer walk in the futility of our own minds but according to the truth, having our minds set and *focused on the Spirit.* When we do this, we prevent the devil from having an opportunity to defeat us in our circumstances.

Proverb 14:16 says that walking after what seems right to us (after our own reason and old strategies) leads to death. This means we will be cut off from experiencing the Lord's abundance and intimacy with Him. Proverb 1:31 tells us that we eat the fruit of our *own* way—the way of those old fleshly strategies—not the fruit of someone else's way! Galatians 6:8 says the same thing; if we sow to (walk after) the flesh, we will reap corruption from our fleshly way, but if we sow to (walk after, be focused on) the Spirit and truth, we will reap eternal life from the Spirit. Eternal life means experiencing a quality of life—Christ's life—now in our life and relationships.

The way to experience abundant life and peace is to have my mind focused on the Spirit and truth in all of life's circumstances. The Word tells us that if we walk with our minds set on the Spirit, we *won't* fulfill the desires of the flesh! Often, this setting of our minds is a battle. *It is always a discipline of faith.*

On the topic of surrendering our strategies, Oswald Chambers, in his book, *Still Higher for His Highest,* said, "We try to lose ourselves and efface ourselves by an effort; Paul did not efface himself by an effort, his interest in himself simply died right out when he became identified with Christ and Him crucified" (p. 109).

Miles Stanford, in his book, *Principles of Spiritual Growth,* made the same point when he quoted William R. Newell, "If we are disappointed in ourselves, then we have believed in ourselves!" (p. 20). In other words, if we are disappointed in ourselves, we have believed in what *we* can *do.* The whole idea is that we do not surrender by *trying* to surrender or by having our minds set on the surrender; rather, they should be set on truth and fellowship with God.

Kay's illustration

I frequently quote my friend Kay Ruff. She says that surrender is not a power struggle, it is a truth struggle. Kay describes surrender with the story of her rehabilitation after knee surgery.

> In a sense, my therapist had become my God during rehabilitation, which was three times a week for ten weeks after my knee replacement surgery. I looked to her for instruction, strength, courage and hope. My goal and desire was to listen, trust and obey for I knew her will was only for my good. I was not offended by some of the seemingly ridiculous things she asked me to do over and over and over again until I could do them well. And then she would add weights to all that I had mastered, which made for some real work.

> You see, the pain in my knee was so constant that I favored that leg. As a result, the muscles had atrophied so that I couldn't bend or extend it properly. Not being able to walk well and not being free from pain prevented me from experiencing real life! The therapist's goal, now that I had a new knee, was not only to strengthen the muscles but also to stretch them. Teaching them to constrict and to relax, which seemed like a contradiction at the

time, was a necessary assignment. I could bend the leg at the knee very little, but as for relaxing it, why, it hadn't been relaxed in over a year and felt like it was set up in concrete.

After a few weeks of therapy, the range of motion in the bending of it was coming along nicely, but the extending just wasn't happening. The hamstring seemed to be frozen in time so I was given specific exercises that targeted that muscle. There was still little success until she laid hands on the back of my knee and gave a deep massage, which was almost unbearable. But after that, little by little I began to be able to relax that muscle on command, with much practice!

It just doesn't sound right, does it ... to practice relaxing. But herein is the key. My therapist knew that to practice anything you must focus. You see, for over a year I had focused on protecting my knee from pain by not moving it, using it as little as possible. Defending and protecting my knee had literally become "life" to me. The muscles had atrophied and were of no use.

Now I have a new knee socket. But it was placed in among those same old muscles with their old habits, and it is the muscles' job to make the knee function. I had already come to a place of surrender when I exchanged my old knee for a new one. There was no doubt about the fact that I had a new knee because I had all the blood, guts and stitches that go with it, and I could see it on the x-ray, brand spanking new and ready to go.

I could go, but would I go? Another major decision was in the making. Would my focus still be on protecting myself from pain by not being willing to use my knee, or would I focus on learning the new way and be willing to experience the pain of it for a short season, to have a life? Relaxing the muscles so my leg could straighten out by letting them rest in a necessary position for maximum function and comfort has been my biggest obstacle.

It is the same way with Christ living His life through me. I will rest not only *from* my old ways but *in* the certainty that Christ can and will operate through me with the power of His resurrection life in thought, word and deed in the ordinary moments of my days as well as the great crises of my life. Going on, focusing on, apprehending Christ as my new LIFE... practicing this, focusing on this, is relaxing the muscles and being surrendered to the Lord.

These illustrations of surrender are pictures of what it means to abide in Christ.

By now, Darryl and Mattie were relaxed and reflective as they considered a new way of looking at surrender to God. I expressed that they were beginning to learn about exercising faith.

Darryl revealed, "After we had that attack of 'road rage,' as you called it, I thought I had even failed at surrender. Now, I think I am beginning to understand that surrender isn't based on my efforts or performance but on *ceasing* from my inner struggle *to do and have* something, to protect myself and just believe God's promises."

"You are absolutely right," I replied. I was grateful he saw this.

What follows is a summary of concepts of surrender and abiding.

Surrender and Abiding

❑ is to relax and *cease from* struggling to satisfy our neediness by *self-reliance and self-effort*
Psalm 46:10; John 15:4,5; Hebrews 4:10

❑ is *not by efforts to put away* the old

❑ is *not* passivity

❑ is like *focusing on learning a new language*
Romans 8:5; Colossians 3:2; Isaiah 50:7

❑ is "to faith"—to intimately *focus on the Spirit and truth, depending* on the Lord and His indwelling life

❑ is "faithing"—an *ongoing process of choices* that are, often moment by moment, disciplines

❑ is to delight ourselves in the Lord and commit our way to Him
Psalm 37:4,5

Our surrender, Christ's life

Many people believe the Christian life and the promises of Christ are to be attained by self-EFFORT of some kind. Our victory in life is experienced by abiding in Christ and resting from our own strategies. This is surrender, and it includes believing the Lord will come through and that He *has given us* the victory. Mattie asked, "Just what does that phrase about God giving us the victory *mean*? I have heard it many times, but it has just sounded so religious."

"Christ won our victory for us by dying on the cross and being resurrected. Dying is opposite of our thinking about how a battle is won. At the same time, his death was the punishment for our sin. He paid the price and won our victory over our sin, Satan and failure and restored us to the place of being in union with God, having every good thing God freely gives. We *have* the victory because we died with Him and we have His life indwelling us," I replied.

This is such powerful truth, it is almost impossible to comprehend—God Himself indwelling our spirit and being our life. He will live that life out through us. **Everything we need is contained within His life.** As His life flows out through us, we and others with whom we come in contact are able to partake of it. When we intimately embrace the Lord and His life, there is healing from emotional pain, wholeness for those who have been broken, freedom for those who have been bound and nurturing for us who were never nurtured.

"The problem is that we don't *experience* that victory—the good things of the abundant life—as long as we depend on ourselves and our focus is on our needs being met by our, or another's, performance. Jesus said that He is the vine and we are branches. The sustaining life that produces fruit is in the vine. Since the branch abides in, or depends on, the vine for its life, we also are to abide or rest in the fact that the Lord will sustain us and live His life through us.

In order to cease from our marital struggles and abide in Christ, we must spend time learning truth, thanking God for it, listening to Him and getting to know Him as our Father. The couples needed to realize that none of us can achieve this life in Christ by fleshly effort or performance because only Christ gives and lives His life.

Remember that abiding is not passivity as some would suppose. It is an active choosing to change beliefs, trust God and behave accordingly in the face of unfairness. Focusing on truth while relinquishing our inner striving to rely on old ways is a discipline of living in grace. We will see in subsequent chapters that it is actually a fight of faith.

The apostle Paul said in Philippians 1:21, "For to me, to live is Christ..." This means that if I experience a full, satisfying, secure, joyful quality of life, it *is* Christ's life living through me. Yes, even in marriage! That is what Galatians 2:20 means when it says,

> *I have been crucified with Christ; it is no longer I who live, but Christ lives in me; and the life which I now live in the flesh I live by the faith of the Son of God, who loved me and gave Himself for me* (NKJV).

Even victory over temptation and sin happens as we allow Him to express His life through us. "God always leads us in triumph in Christ" (2 Corinthians 2:14), and in whatever things happen to us, "We are more than conquerors through Him who loved us" (Romans 8:37).

Our emotional neediness being satisfied and our power to live successfully in marriage is the result of choosing to relinquish our strategies as we rely on Christ to live His life out through us as we relate with our spouse. Even He said that He did nothing on His own initiative. And neither can we.

Stone and Smith say in *The Rest of the Gospel,*

> It is impossible for a person to know their union with Christ, and live out of that union, if they don't know that they have died with Christ. If I think the old me is still alive, I am still my point of reference. I am still trying to correct me, straighten me up, make something out of me, or do something to change me. As long as the emphasis is on me, it can't be on Christ in me. So I am a divided person (p. 126).

Occasionally I will ask couples in counseling to look up the following Scriptures for homework. These Scriptures show that it is Christ who will live His life through you. This is the same homework I assigned to Darryl and Mattie. *You may wish to fill in the blanks with the correct Scriptures. This can help reinforce the truth that it is Christ who must live a victorious life through you in your relationship with your spouse.*

Christ in you will perform the work:

So you must remember that your maturity in Christ and your living in relationship with your spouse must be done:
not by _____ nor by _____ but by _____
(Zechariah 4:6).

It is the **life of Christ** indwelling you that will fulfill you and love through you. Christ is your victory because you have His life.
God gives us the _____ through _____
_____ (1 Corinthians 15:57). _____ is able
to do exceeding abundantly beyond all that we ask or think according to
_____ (Ephesians 3:20).
"Faithful is He who calls you, and **He** also will _____"
(1 Thessalonians 5:24). "**He** who began a good work in you will
_____" (Philippians 1:6). Christ
said, "_____" (John 15:5).

The following quotation is an easy reference to recalling the truth that it is Christ who must live His life through us if we are to experience freedom and the abundance. Credit is given to whomever came up with it!

Christ's *Life*

He gave *His life* for us
to
Give *His life* to us
to
Live *His life* through us.

■ **Christ is *your life*** (your power and victory) (Colossians 3:4).

■ **For you to *live*** (being an "overcomer," and having needs met) **is Christ** (Philippians 1:21).

■ **You are saved** (your emotions, your mind and well-being, etc.) **by *His life*** (Romans 5:10).

Even though Mattie was receiving these truths, she was still struggling as she said, "I hear what you're saying, but the simple things get to me. It's the unfairness of having the responsibility of remembering what needs to be done, suggesting and reminding. For example, we have lived in our house ten years and Darryl *still* has to *ask* where the peanut butter is!"

I told Mattie that she must quit struggling, kicking against unfairness, trying to prove her point, and trying to "fix." She must drop her end of the rope and trust that God is who He says He is for her. In *The Rest of the Gospel,* Stone and Smith call trusting God living in the unseen eternal realm. We who are united with Christ can choose to walk in the unseen world of the Holy Spirit where there is security and certainty or we can live in the world of the seen where there is neediness, things change and nothing is secure.

When we talk religiously and say, "I know God is my sufficiency *but* I don't really have all I need," or "I know that God promised me wisdom *but* all I have is confusion," Stone and Smith call this "living in junk." They say we need to live putting the *but* where it belongs. We should be stating that we feel we lack and THEN put God's truth *after* the *but*. For example, "It is so unjust how my spouse puts me down and ignores me, *but* I know Christ is my peace, the protector of my heart and He is my joy. Then the "but" becomes what they call the "holy *but*."

Darryl had a question. "If we aren't to rely on ourselves anymore but totally on Christ, where do our natural abilities come in?" Darryl had prided himself in his knowledge and reason.

I said, "Jesus was perfect and yet He repeatedly said that *He* did *nothing* on His own initiative (John 5:30; 7:16; 8:28; 8:42; 12:49). He also said that without Him *we* can do *nothing.* In our own abilities, we can do nothing that is lasting or that brings God's fulfillment. Steve McVey says in *Grace Rules,* 'Ability becomes a liability when we trust in the ability instead of trusting in God.' Steve also reminds us that 'you can't *achieve* victory in the Christian life, you can only *receive* it'" (p. 40).

Tony and Katrina: Stuck!

Tony leaned forward. His elbows on his knees and fingers interlocked, he stared down at his muddy boots from behind his gold-rimmed glasses. Katrina, with her porcelain-like complexion, fingered her hoop earrings and stared at her lap. Her foot did not jiggle today, but both were still stuck on their journey and not ready to cross the river even though I had given them the illustrations on surrender and trusting Christ.

Nevertheless, they wanted to continue with the counseling process because, as Katrina said, "We believe this is the truth and we think we have made progress." They had been to several other counselors where they had been given behavioral assignments that did not bring lasting change in their relationship.

In one of their sessions, I was discussing the truth that each of them is complete in Christ and it is His desire that they *experience* this completeness as He lives His life through them.

Tony suddenly said, "I thought Katrina and I were supposed to complete each other! If what you say is true, then why do we get married? What is the purpose?"

The question gave me the opportunity to explain that the purpose of marriage is so we can find true intimacy. "That is confusing! What do you mean?" quizzed Tony. I gave them the "piano illustration," explaining that as each partner comes to know God intimately, there is true intimacy with each other.

Tony's next question was, "What if only one of us comes to that place of intimacy with God?" His question was born out of his fear of never achieving the satisfaction from attachment with Katrina and her attention and respect. To him, Katrina was totally emotionally absent from him. Tony was also still struggling with believing he must have respect from her to fill his role as husband and feel of worth as a man.

I remarked that if only one partner chooses surrender, then the Lord would use the marriage relationship to bring *that* mate to dependence on God and to the experience of God's fulfillment within the couple relationship.

I responded to his question with the following comment from Jan Silvious' book, *Moving beyond the Myths*. Her remarks are directed to wives but are just as true for husbands. I had also read this quote in Mattie and Darryl's counseling when Mattie said that the thing she had to have to be okay was for Darryl to validate and cherish her.

> A wife must realize her life does not rest on her husband's adoration, acceptance, or understanding. Her future is not tied to his abilities, or ingenuity. Her emotional, spiritual, and physical well-being are her responsibility alone. If he fulfills the role of a "virtuous husband," then she is blessed. If he does not, then she is still blessed. She may be challenged, but in that challenge there is still a blessing. It is all in her perspective. In fact, that is true with everything that happens to us. It is that well-worn axiom: It is not what happens to us that matters, but what we think about what happens to us (p. 92).

I must explain that this quote *does not mean* a mate should *not* adore, respect and seek to understand the other! It *does* mean one is not to *depend* on his partner's giving these things in order to be satisfied and fulfilled because in doing so, there will definitely be emotional pain, disappointment and resentment.

Tony and Katrina stared blankly at me. Finally, he said, "I don't understand. Marriage should be a place where two people love each other. Why would God allow us to deal with all the hurtful, unfair situations?"

"Marital partners certainly *should* love and honor each other!" I said, "The fact is, they do not always do this. I am going to help you learn how love should be practiced in marriage. But first, I want to answer your question about why God allows painful circumstances in marriage."

This would also answer Mattie's comment and her request, which had been, "Anne, you said it was no accident when two opposites marry and can't give what the other needs. Please explain why the Lord allows these painful differences between marital couples."

Chapter 14

Roadblocks: Adversity, But *Why?*

> **On the Map:** In the wilderness or in Canaan. Trials and oppositions are ongoing in life and in marriage. They come to us throughout our lifelong journey from Egypt through the wilderness area and after we have crossed the Jordan river and dwell in Canaan. The Lord desires that fleshly provocations and misunderstandings be the opportunity for us to partake of His victory and blessings within our marital relationship.

We live on a little hill far from the city lights with clear views of the sky. A precocious four-year-old who was visiting us stepped out into the cold night air on our front porch. Her breath sharply inhaled in an automatic response to an immense canopy of bright stars as she exclaimed, "Ohhh...I haven't seen stars like this!" When we pointed out a brilliant Venus in the western sky, she responded with, "Quick, shut your eyes real tight! We need to wish upon that star! Star light, star bright, first star I see tonight. I wish I may, I wish I might have this wish I wish tonight!"

Most of us, I think, have wished to God, hoping He would give us the right person or the things we want without the adversity life brings. We believe that if He does, we will live happily ever after. Sometimes, *our prayers are much like this wish* of the sweet four-year-old. We wish and worry to God, not understanding His way or how His promises are to be experienced.

I related how Darryl and Mattie experienced what I call, "road rage," on their journey. This attack was typical of the conflicts that initially brought them to counseling. Even after each made the choice to surrender to God and rely on Him, they "blew it" as they went.

It is not unusual for a couple to be progressing well for a while and then unexpectedly have a setback. The old patterns may resurface for a few days—perhaps over a weekend. If this happens, sometimes I have had them return to a session and say, "It is all over!" It feels to them as if there has been no growth when actually there has been much progress in their walk together. And I have to remind them of that.

Since they are in God's training process, so to speak, they learn to refocus on the truth, re-discipline and move forward again. These hurtful situations will become less frequent as time goes by and they learn to walk in their victory in Christ. Darryl and Mattie had needed the additional teaching on surrender and needed to know that Christ would live out His life through them as they give up on their perceived entitlements and defenses. On "The Map," they had just arrived in Canaan where surrender would need to be ongoing. Recall that the word *canaan* means "surrender."

As they traveled, the individuals had felt as if there had been continuous roadblocks to their goals of finding *Contentment, Security, Worth* and validation in marriage. Darryl and Mattie, as well as Tony and Katrina, had unanswered questions about *why* God allows roadblocks—the painful difficulties between couples—and how God intends to use these conflicts couples have in marriage. They didn't realize that the answer to their question about why God allows adversity in marriage and the concept of surrender would have a connection.

Why *would* the Lord allow pain and disappointments in marriage? Why *are* there painful differences between spouses? Why *do* we marry those who resist and demean us? Could there be valid *reasons* we are uncomfortable with our spouse's ways? How does the Lord purpose to use the conflicts? The couples were ready to hear the answers.

Trials and Adversity

The subject of "trials and adversity" brings feelings of resistance in most of us. Many believe a good God wouldn't allow pain. Others have been taught that obstacles and oppositions should be averted, rebuked or managed in such a way that they no longer plague us.

Tony spoke from his hurt. He was forceful, "I never have even imagined that God's intentions in trials and adversity could have anything to do with *marriage!*"

When aggravations, obstacles, injustices or even fiery ordeals happen in marriage and there is unresolved conflict, we are puzzled and can't believe this strange thing is happening to us. We wonder how God could possibly be involved in our difficulties. We know something isn't right and we set out to try to fix whatever it is and change our mate.

Every married couple will experience roadblocks, injustices and disappointments on their journey. When they come for marital counseling, they are stuck and struggling in response to these unfair situations. One can often understand if a person suffers because of some sin or immorality in his own life, but to suffer unjustly seems so unacceptable. All want relief and relief is God's desire for His people, *but it comes in a way that is opposite than most would think.*

It's very true that marital partners *should* be walking in love, mutually respecting and caring for each other. But people *will* walk after the flesh until they begin to mature in Christ and there *will be* selfishness and the old patterns of trying to make life work. The way of fleshly strategies is that they just naturally produce trials, strife and pain as people relate.

We are attracted to and marry a partner who turns out to be unable to give us the very things we need and want the most. *The areas in which one spouse is the neediest and puts the most fleshly demands on the other correspond to the very areas in which the other spouse finds it most difficult to give of him/herself after the flesh. This is no accident, because these situations become the opportunities the Lord uses to frustrate us to the place of yielding our demands and strategies!* These circumstances are tailored and orchestrated by God to be what we need to push us toward surrender. You may want to refer back to the chart entitled, "Some Typical Combinations of Marital Partners" to observe the truth in this statement.

> We are attracted to and marry a partner who turns out to be unable to give us what we need and want the most. The areas in which one spouse is the most needy and puts the most fleshly demands on the other correspond to the very areas in which the other spouse finds it most difficult to give of him/herself after the flesh. *This is no accident, because these situations become the opportunities the Lord would use to frustrate us to the place of yielding our demands and strategies!* These circumstances are tailored and orchestrated by God to be what is needed to push us toward surrender.

Relational combinations illustrating how one person's flesh can become the other's "trial":

There may be various combinations of fleshly attachments such as the following. Notice that the very characteristic we are attracted to in a person often becomes the source of frustrations later! The following combinations are only examples. There are many others.

FLESH	FLESH
Super Responsible Controls situations/people to feel SECURE, of WORTH. *Belief: I must be responsible to be secure and maintain a sense of worth.*	**Irresponsible/Passive-aggressive** Blocks being controlled, to find PEACE. Doesn't try, to avoid failure (WORTH). *Belief: I must avoid being controlled to find peace. I must be catered to, to know I am of value.*
Dominant Controller/Distancer Controls to have his way (a getter); doesn't give. To validate WORTH. *Belief: I must be right, must be heard and things must go my way to validate my worth.*	**Co-dependent/Pleaser/Pursuer** Smothering. Controls by "fixing," rescuing and "pleasing" for APPRECIATION, WORTH. *Belief: I must fix and/or please others for love and acceptance and avoid rejection. I must be heard to know I am of worth.*
Steady, Quiet, Reserved Controls self and situations for SECURITY, PEACE. *Belief: I must stay guarded to be safe. Finances will bring security.*	**Outgoing/Reactive/Verbose** Tries to control by criticizing and often uses self-pity in an effort to find ACCEPTANCE. Is social, talkative, to find WORTH. *Belief: My spouse must talk about feelings for me to feel accepted and find worth.*
Organized/Serious/Logical Controls to find CONTENTMENT, WORTH. *Belief: I must follow the rules to be content and maintain worth.*	**Disorganized/Carefree/Subjective** Tries to avoid rules and being controlled to maintain a sense of WORTH. *Belief: I must have what I want and avoid being controlled to know I am of value.*

As we travel on our trip, the instruments God allows to break our self-preserving ways range from small interruptions to our not getting our way, to our partner's irresponsibility, to our not being heard, not respected and so on. God may even use a mate's involvement in substance abuse or an affair to bring a person to a place of laying down his old strategies. If you are wondering, God doesn't have to manufacture and send these trials to marital couples! He merely *orchestrates what is already there* in our mate as he/she walks after the flesh to frustrate us and bring us to the end of our struggling to have our fleshly way. And if you wonder how to know something in you is *fleshly*, if you are bitter and hold grudges when you are slighted or don't get your way, it is your *flesh* that has been offended.

Our marital trial can be the characteristic in our mate that prevents us from getting our neediness satisfied in the way we want. **It doesn't have to be anything major.** The Lord allows this, of course, because He wants us to be *broken of our ineffective ways* in exchange for dependency on Him to meet our needs perfectly. Sometimes we refer to this as our arriving at a place of *brokenness*.

Darryl and Mattie are typical of many of us. When they learned that their strategies weren't working, they chose to surrender. But since there was an attack of road-rage, it is likely they had not been ready at that time to allow the *breaking* of their *willful self-effort*. We can be very strong in our flesh, in our walking independently from God. We don't see it as that because our self-preserving ways can look so good and even seem religious.

Tony and Katrina were still having conflicts, and when I began to explain why God doesn't prevent these misunderstandings, Katrina was restless and emphatic in her stinging remarks. "Well, I have said in the past that I see Tony's criticisms and accusations as emotional abuse. And I have been told that if it is emotional abuse, God gives us an out."

I had to tell Katrina that I knew of no scriptural grounds for divorce in such cases. And the truth is, the Word of God is very absolute in stressing that the Lord is our shelter in the storm. It is very clear that Christ came to be our safety and to bring protection and healing for our soul— our mind and emotions. We are to experience the reality of this as we choose to take refuge in Him. If there were no trials, we wouldn't have to make these choices of the heart and exercise faith.

This does not mean someone has to stay in ongoing physical or emotional *violence*. I have not met any Christians who have arrived at a place of enduring in faith while in a continuously violent situation. Separation can be advised in a situation such as this—with much prayer and fasting. The Christian partner's response in such a circumstance must be the attitude of Christ. One's response cannot be from manipulation or revenge.

When we resist our trial, we *detour* around the very thing the Lord would use to work us *into* surrender, abiding in Him and being conformed to Christ's image (His attitude or likeness). In other words, we resist being intimately "attuned" to Him. Remember the piano illustration? We must *receive* the adverse circumstance as God's instrument to break our hold on our independent strategies and attitudes. Otherwise, day after day we can resolve to surrender, focus on Christ's promises and, still, nothing changes in us; we continue our journey on empty: unfulfilled, without joy or peace. Christ learned obedience by the things He suffered. And God's design is the same for us. We are to follow this way of Jesus. We must be brought to the point of being broken of confidence in our own abilities to manage life and our marital relationship.

Jeff Van Vonderan asked the question, "Why would God 'fix' your spouse if you are looking to your spouse to fulfill you and bring you satisfaction?" It is through our frustration of trying to get our spouse to change that we can see the futility of trying to obtain satisfaction by our tremendous self-efforts. **We must receive our mates as they are and stop trying to change them.** *Mr. Van Vonderan says that God wants us to see that we can't get by self-effort what He gives for free.*

In 1 Peter 4:12–19, we are told to not be surprised when the fiery trial comes.

These Scriptures tell us that testing and difficulties will come to all beginning with the household of God and it is to be expected. And believe it or not, in these verses we are told that God's purpose in testing—the outcome of it—is that we would experience His blessings and promises! The fire of adversity, in marriage or in any other situation, will have an end result of either perfecting us and bringing us God's best, or we can allow it to devastate us. ***The outcome is based on our response.***

In counseling I frequently have people tell me they are reluctant to surrender because they fear that, if they do, God will bring more intense trials. Scripture teaches that trials will come to all anyway. We will have adversity all our lives *whether we surrender or not. Surrender actually brings relief to our internal dilemmas.* Peace comes when we respond in faith.

Kay Ruff so aptly said, "When God allows stress to increase, often beyond one's endurance, it is to wean us off of our love affair with our flesh." She continued, "We must go through Gethsemane as Jesus Christ did on His way to the cross. It is a place of personal agony to bring us to a choice of the will. It comes down to a place of surrender. *When you surrender everything, you have nothing else to fear, because you then have nothing to lose.*"

> Kay Ruff so aptly said, "When God allows stress to increase, often beyond one's endurance, it is to wean us off of our love affair with our fleshly strategies." She continued, "We must go through Gethsemane as Jesus Christ did on His way to the cross. It is a place of personal agony to bring us to a choice of the will. It comes down to a place of surrender. *When you surrender everything, you have nothing else to fear, because you then have nothing to lose.*"

In answering the questions about why the Lord allows our mate's imperfections to be a test or a trial for us, we must consider what God's intention was in the trials Christ faced. We are to learn from Christ's example for us, that is, His attitude in response to the adversity that came against Him. We are to observe the *outcome* of His response as well. It may be surprising to discover that when we allow *our* response or attitude toward trials to be the same as Christ's, a victorious outcome will also be ours. In the next chapter, I will explain more about this attitude or mind-set of Christ.

It was injustice that took Christ to the cross and to His voluntarily laying down His rights as God. Out of rejection, false accusation, being misunderstood, despised, humiliated and being crucified, came resurrection life and power. His willingness to go through a process that led to death was the key to His victory *over* death and defeat. Christ's victory over the enemy and over death did not come from just walking through the adversity itself, but it came from His *response* to it. And it must be the same with us if we are to experience His love and power within marriage. This is the great *paradox* of Christianity! life springing up out of death is a great mystery and the opposite of human reason.

Often we have been told that in order to know Him, we must get to know about His character. This is true. But this is, by far, not all. **To know Christ means to know Him in His attitude and experience.** *Scripture says if we are to know Him in His resurrection power as we live life, we must know Him in the fellowship of His suffering, being conformed to His death. This means having our response to trials molded to be like His response to trials and injustices; His cross* (Philippians 3:10). The *knowing* God that the Scripture speaks of has the intensity and intimacy of meaning as a husband knowing his wife sexually—in the most intimate way possible; although there is, of course, no sexual connotation in the scriptural reference of our knowing God.

Mike Mason, in his award-winning book, *The Mystery of Marriage*, says that one of the chief characteristics of love is that it asks for everything. Not just a little bit, or a whole lot, but everything. He spoke from his own experience when he said how hard that is. He said,

> The wedding is merely the beginning of a lifelong process of handing over absolutely everything, and not simply everything one owns but everything one is. There is no one who is not broken by this process. It is excruciating and inexorable, and no one can stand up to it.

He also says that everyone comes to ruin by it. Either our flesh is ruined by it, or those who run from it will themselves come to ruin and remain defeated with a wound that never heals (pp. 15,16).

Tony interrupted me, "I don't know what to say about all of this. It is hard to get away from the belief that men are not supposed to be weak or even look weak. So what does this mean for me, for each of us, in our marriage?"

Praying for the Lord to speak to their hearts, I replied, "You must simply let go of your old ways and depend on God's truth as you live in your relationship with each other, because the old strategies *block* the good things God wants to satisfy you with.

"Our old strategies and entitlements we have regarding marriage are like the chaff that surrounds a grain of wheat. The chaff blocks the good part of the wheat and must be broken away before the wheat can be used. The chaff is the strategies formed in us as children that must be denied or put away if godly maturity is to come (Matthew 5:15; 13:12; 1 Corinthians 13:11). The purpose of the storm (trial) is to carry away the chaff (Job 21:18), and yet God is our refuge from the storm (Isaiah 25:4)! He is the calm *within* the storm. It takes humility to depend on Him as your refuge but when you do, *the storm within you will be calmed.*

"**Tony, you must humble yourself in order to let go of presumed "rights" and focus on truth in the midst of the unfairness in your relationship.** When you *humble* yourself, *anxiety and fear will go* (1 Peter 5:6–7). The root of anxiety, self-pity, jealousy, resistance and hurt feelings is pride—the pride of believing *our way is the right way* for emotional security, fulfillment and joy to be experienced. Since humility is the opposite of pride, surrender in the face of unfairness will be humbling. But the result will be that *the peace of God will guard your hearts and minds* (Philippians 4:7). Humbling yourselves means, for example, being willing to look wrong even when you are right."

Mike Mason says, "Matrimony launches a fierce and unrelenting attack upon the fortress of the ego, upon that place in a person which craves privacy, independence, self-sufficiency" (p. 17). And, I would add, upon that place that craves attention and respect.

We do have a love affair with old strategies and self-protections. But they dam off the river of living water within us, preventing it from flowing out, filling and *permeating us* so that we, as well as others, can drink of it. When we allow ourselves to be emptied of our strategies and give ourselves up for the other, the life of Christ in our Spirit flows out and fills us. We will be filled with His Spirit! We will be filled and

150

empowered as wind fills a sail to carry a boat along. We have a magnificent inheritance for this life and we can enjoy it now in marriage, in a vocation and with others if we allow our fleshly reliance to be broken and respond with the mind-set of Christ. This is the first purpose God has for allowing the unfairness, the hard times, the adversity in our relationships. It brings us to a true love affair with our mate and God.

This is what the Apostle Paul meant when he said, "I die daily" (1 Corinthians 15:31). This is what Jesus meant when he said, **"If anyone wishes to come after Me, he must deny himself, and take up his cross and follow Me"** (Matthew 16:24). *It is impossible to take up our cross (trial) without denying ourselves.* You can't have one without the other This is also what Scripture means when it says we must lose our (fleshly) life to find (Christ's) life (Matthew 10:38,39).

Jesus said that whoever doesn't take up his cross *cannot* be His disciple (Luke 14:26,27). To instill hope, the psalmist David said that the righteous one who trusts God will have many trials, but the Lord delivers him out of them all (Psalm 34:19). But if we live after the old fleshly strategies, we will die (Romans 8:13). *In other words, if we don't die to (or deny) the flesh, we will die emotionally!*

This in no way means *asceticism* or denying one's self *things* and being a martyr. That kind of thinking is an end in itself and has no place in Christianity. I am referring to an attitude of the heart that results in our experiencing, in marriage and all of life's circumstances, every good thing that has been given us in Christ Jesus. I will soon describe more specifically this heart attitude, which was Christ's mind-set to the injustices of life.

Anything we thought we would gain by our old ways is like trash. It has never, and will never, satisfy us for long. We must focus on the joy that is up ahead of us as we receive our cross despising the shame of it—the same as Christ did. Joy, satisfaction and peace *will* come to us as we live in our marriage.

Receiving Your Mate

"You are created for relationship with God and with others," I said to Tony and Katrina. "This Christian life of which I speak has to be lived out in relationships. You cannot be isolated and live this life. The first place it should become a reality for you is within your marriage.

"You must *receive* your mate with his/her imperfections. You must receive your mate as a gift from God, knowing that the things you would change were allowed by Him for a purpose. It is to perfect you and mold you into a vehicle through which the glory of God will be revealed. It is to conform you into Christ's likeness, His attitude.

"Receiving breaks down barriers and actually frees both you and your partner. In accepting your spouse as he/she is, you show sacrificial love and grace. To do this, you must humble yourself and sacrifice your old life with its beliefs that things be right and fair. You must learn to let down your guard and not hide your weaknesses. *This brings intimacy with the Lord and with your mate.* The Word says that no person has any greater love than to lay down his fleshly life for his friend (John 15:13).

"It will feel humiliating to accept your partner with his/her critical, ignoring or irritating ways, but this is a discipline or training for the purpose of sharing in Christ's holiness. By this, you can press on to maturity and run your race with faith and patience (Hebrews 6:1, 12; 12:1,2, 7–1). The great news is that *a test doesn't last forever.* There will be other tests, but in time, your focusing on truth and responding correctly to the tests can become more automatic.

"Godliness and maturity in Christ and personal fulfillment can only be experienced through this training process. In fact, we are told that all who desire to be godly will be persecuted or treated unjustly for the purpose of bringing out Christ's holiness through us (2 Timothy 3:12; Matthew 5:10; Philippians 1:24). In other words, we must drink of the same cup and be baptized with the same baptism as Christ.

"Surrender is lived out in marriage by receiving your mate as you sacrifice yourself. This is the sacrifice of becoming weak *in your own* strength as you receive uncomfortable situations," I explained. Christ's power or strength is made perfect in us in our weakness (2 Corinthians 12:9).

Some of us may respond as Katrina did, "But I *am* weak and incapable and at others' mercy." A person may *look and feel* weak, but even for those who feel this way such as the people-pleaser, the victim, the dependent or non-decisive person or the blamer, living out of their old strategies *becomes* their strength and self-protection! They are strong in these strategies and must relinquish them to enjoy God's best.

Jesus tells us we can gain the things of the world if we live by our own demands of what we think is right and just for us, but we will forfeit our own souls (minds, emotions) in the process. We will also cause ourselves to be wounded by sorrows and fear. But if we deny ourselves and take up our cross, we will find our life (Christ's life). We will find within marriage that which frees, nurtures, empowers, sustains and satisfies. And it will come from God (Matthew 16: 24–26).

Steve and Valerie Bell, in their book, *Made to be Loved,* say that we fight about "who's on top; who brings the most to the marriage, or who got the better deal" while we keep score (p. 126). They say that grace and sacrificial love is not denying that a spouse is disrespectful, but it is to accept them and give of one's self in return. When we do this we practice obedience to God, and holiness. To do this is true worship and brings that experience of intimacy with God and one's mate.

In *The Release of the Spirit*, Watchman Nee said, the Lord "wants to break our outward man in order that the inward man (Christ) may have a way out!" (p. 10–11). Without this crucifixion, we will never learn to love, we will never experience His power and we will never experience the fulfilling of our needs. We must be willing for the chaff of our self-will to be broken away before we can walk in His resurrection power. Second Corinthians 1:9 says that this happens so that we won't trust ourselves but God instead.

We have this treasure (Christ) in our earthly bodies so that the surpassing greatness of the power (experienced in our lives) may be of God and not from ourselves (2 Corinthians 4:7). In 2 Corinthians 4:11, we are told that "we who live are constantly being delivered over to death for Jesus' sake, so that the life of Jesus also may be manifested in our mortal flesh." Surrender in the face of injustice, unfairness and fear may *feel* like death, but the outcome will be life! This is astounding truth and that paradox of which I spoke.

In my booklet, *The Purpose of Trials and Adversity*, you can find a more complete teaching on the subject with Scripture references.

Following, I have summarized from the booklet some of the results in us when we receive our test with the mind-set of Christ:

1. We will be perfect (mature) and complete, lacking nothing.

2. We will be strengthened, confirmed and established.

3. Christ's power will be revealed through us through our mortal flesh.

4. Patience will have been worked in us.

5. We will be partakers of His holiness (which already indwells us as believers).

6. We will be found in peace.

7. We will be found to be righteousness (it will be revealed through us).

8. We will be found to be blameless (it will be evident).

9. We will receive the crown of life.

10. We will know experientially our reign with Christ.

11. We will experience the salvation of our soul (mind, emotions).

12. We will be revealed as being of His household.

13. We will be transformed by the renewing of our minds.

14. We will have joy.

15. We will partake of His promises.

16. We will be filled with His fullness.

17. Fear will be cast out.

18. We will bear the fruit of the Spirit.

It was January 9, 2001. As the Presidential Inaugural parade passed, a protestor shouted loudly and raised his sign that read, "Why did the loser win?" He was referring to the voting dilemma in Florida during which the other party believed they won. But the protestor expressed a paradoxical truth he did not understand. And that is, in the kingdom of

God and the unseen realm in which Christians must live, the spiritual truth is that we must lose to win and lose to find. A few minutes later during the Inaugural Address, President George W. Bush seemed to answer the protestor as he quoted these words, "The race is not to the swift nor the battle to the strong" (Ecclesiastes 9: 11).

We must remember that it is "not by might nor by power, but by My Spirit said the LORD of hosts" (Zechariah 4:6a). According to Romans 9:15,16, our experiencing God's compassion and mercy does not depend on our control, on what *we* can do, not on our will, nor on our running or striving, but on God. Living by the world's principles offers a promise that never delivers.

Following are several Scriptures I shared with the couples on losing our fleshly life and then promises of what we will find as a result. I explained that we would soon talk about what it would "look like" in the marriage.

We Must Lose to Find

Losing

Scriptural evidences that we must lose dependency on our old soulish life and strategies, relinquishing our perceived entitlements in marriage and other relationships in life:

- ❑ We must choose to *lose our life, or die daily* (Matthew 16:25, Luke 17:33).

- ❑ The grain of wheat (we) must *fall into the ground and die* (John 12:24).

- ❑ When we become mature, we *do away with childish things* (1 Corinthians 13:11).

- ❑ We must *leave dependency on house, lands (material things), mothers, fathers (relationships)* (Mark 10:29–30).

- ❑ We must *deny ourselves, take up our cross* (Matthew 16:24).

- ❑ It is necessary that we *sell all we have* (Matthew 13:46, Mark 10:21).

- ❑ We are to no longer walk in the *futility of own minds* (myths) or lean on our *own understanding* (Ephesians 4:17).

❑ We must *forget those things that lie behind* (Philippians 3:13).

❑ It is necessary that we *cease, or rest from, our own works* (our strategies) (Hebrews 4:9–10).

❑ We must be content in our *weaknesses* (2 Corinthians 12:10).

❑ We are to put *no confidence* in our flesh (Philippians 3:3).

❑ When we walk in the Spirit (denying fleshly strategies) we *won't carry out the desire of the flesh* (Galatians 5:16).

❑ It is necessary to *turn from our own way, speaking our own words* (our strategies) (Isaiah 58:13).

❑ We must not make *any provision for the flesh* (Romans 13:14).

❑ We are to not *seek our own (fleshly) way* (1 Corinthians 13:5).

❑ We must *sow ourselves (our own way) to the Spirit* (Galatians 6:7).

❑ It is necessary to *humble ourselves* under the mighty hand of God (1 Peter 5:6, James 4:10).

❑ We must *go by this small gate and narrow way* (Matthew 7:1).

Finding

Scriptural promises of FINDING Christ's life and provision in our marriage, or other relationships, when we lose dependency our own fleshly life

❑ We will *find our life (Christ's life in us)* (Matthew 16:25).

❑ We will *produce fruit* of the Spirit (Galatians 5:22, John 15:5, 12:24).

❑ We will *become mature* in Christ (1 Corinthians 13:11b).

❑ We will *obtain the "pearl of great price"* (Matthew 13:46).

❑ We will *delight ourselves in the Lord, ride on the heights of the earth and be fed by God* (Isaiah 58:13,14).

❑ We will *have joy* (1 Peter 4:13, Galatians 5:22, Hebrews 12:2).

❑ We *will gain new strength and mount up with wings like eagles. We will run and not get tired, walk and not become weary* (Isaiah 40:31).

❑ We will be *given the hidden wealth of secret places* (Isaiah 4 5:2).

❑ We will *ask whatever we wish and will receive* (John 15:7, 1 John 3:22).

❑ The Lord's *power will be perfected in us* (2 Corinthians 12:10).

❑ We will be *strengthened, perfected, confirmed and established by God* (1 Peter 5:10).

❑ *Christ's life will be revealed in us* (Colossians 3:4).

❑ His *life (our light) will break out like the morning and will be manifest in our MORTAL bodies* (2 Corinthians 4:11).

❑ We will be *experience the Lord's protection* (Isaiah 58:8, Psalm 91:11, 1 Samuel 17:47).

❑ *God will make our paths straight* (Proverbs 3:5).

❑ *When we walk, our steps won't be impeded, and if we run we won't stumble* (Proverb 4:12, Isaiah 45:2a).

❑ We will *experience our needs being supplied* (Philippians 4:19).

❑ We will *be exalted in the proper time* (1 Peter 5:6).

❑ We will *be like trees that will yield fruit in our season, our leaf will not wither, and whatever we do will prosper* (Psalm 1:3).

❑ We *will delight ourselves in an abundance of peace* (KJV) *and be kept in perfect peace* (Psalm 37:11, Isaiah 26:3, Philippians: 4:7).

❑ We *will not be anxious* (I1 Peter 5:6,7).

❑ We *will enter into rest* (contentment) (Hebrews 4:10).

❑ We *will experience the Lord lifting us up* (James 4:10).

❏ We will be *trees of righteousness that will bring forth fruit in our season, our leaf will not wither,* and *whatever we do will prosper* (Psalm 1:3).

❏ We will *find (Christ's) life* within (Matthew 7:14).

Tony's and Katrina's Responses

Tony's suntanned face seemed to pale. He sat up straight, no longer in his laid-back position with his arm across the back of my sofa. His soft brown eyes were serious behind his gold-rimmed glasses. Upon hearing all these paradoxical truths of losing to find, he said, "To think this way will be *radical.* I will need to understand how to not be drawn away by my emotions. When Katrina shuts me out or shows preference to someone else over me, I feel such anger and frustration that sometimes I actually think I might cry. I hate to admit it." He said, "I've felt if I quit struggling and hurting, it would mean I don't care about our relationship." I answered that soon I would be coaching and encouraging them in not living out of their emotions.

Katrina's nervous foot was still. She no longer avoided looking directly at me. She spoke softly and hesitatingly, "The Christian life is not what I had thought. I've always believed I had to hold my spouse accountable and that I was entitled to what God has commanded him to do in marriage.

"But I believe what you are saying is true. I can see that even though Tony's reactions to me have been unfair and I feared what he might do to me, I must learn to trust the Lord to protect me emotionally. I will have to view Tony's criticisms as opportunities for me to surrender and live in obedience to God. I don't have any other option than to live in the same continual distress if I refuse. I am so tired, I think I am about ready to surrender. But Anne, you will have to help direct me through this. Show me *and* Tony how to live beyond our emotions."

I was extremely encouraged to hear they had come to this place.

Latoya's Response

Latoya looked beautiful with her black eyes, coffee-and-cream complexion and hair pulled tightly back from her face. But when she first heard these truths, she sat straight, fixed and on guard as she did in her first counseling session.

For a woman who learned early to be strong, in control and independent to survive and rise above oppression and injustice, all of this was extreme thinking. Accepting injustice, false accusation and oppositions as her cross—instruments to bring surrender of her old ways—was opposite to everything she had ever heard. But God's Spirit in her confirmed this was the truth of experiencing life in Christ. She gradually relaxed as God's Spirit spoke to her heart.

I had to explain to Latoya that living these truths is an attitude of the heart, and it didn't mean that she couldn't work to change things in society that should be changed. But now, she would be free and fulfilled in Christ and could work in all of her undertakings from His wisdom and mind-set.

Even though Joe had chosen not to participate in counseling, *she* needed to experience God's best for her as she lived in her situation. She had found long ago that all attempts to change Joe were exercises in futility. She applied herself to homework and came to surrender after much prayer and diligent examination of the Scriptures.

Walking in the truth would be a learning process for Latoya as it is with everyone else. As she began to "risk" losing her life to find her needs met in Christ's life, she discovered she was placing less demands on herself and on Joe as the weeks went by and she had more peace than ever before. However, strong disagreements were expressed by her close friends and family over her new way of thinking and relating. We will return later to observe more of Latoya's journey.

Darryl's and Mattie's Responses

With her hands neatly folded in her lap, Mattie's words were precise, "I have been in church all my life and years ago heard bits and pieces about taking up our cross and denying ourselves, but I had never understood it. Now that it is being explained, I know I must accept from my heart the very thing I have feared most—painful situations. I don't think I am the only one who has wanted to avoid pain and has tried to see to it that things go calmly," she said.

159

Mattie continued, "This isn't related to marriage, but I think it is significant. I had an open house this past Christmas. I had worked for weeks preparing for it. My sisters and I had struggled to make things perfect for my friends. I thought everything was the best it could be, even the food. I was elated! And do you know, I could hardly believe how suddenly my emotions crashed. I was devastated when I overheard several guests criticizing my decorating! I still am reeling and hurt from the rejection I felt."

"You have been *trying to find life*, acceptance and validation from your friends based on your performance. *This is what was precious to you.* This is the same thing that has happened in your marriage," I responded. "The area of our greatest disappointment in marriage is the very area in which we try the hardest to find life, get our needs met."

Kay Ruff would say that Mattie, like herself, had spent a lifetime stamping out surprises and suffering in an attempt to feel emotionally safe and find approval. Kay has said the very area in which we struggle to win—in which we fight the hardest in *our own* strength to get what we want—will eventually become the source of our greatest pain and defeat.

Strong, resistant Darryl, who had kept a safe distance from Mattie, interjected, "I have resisted Mattie's criticisms and being controlled by her. I have withdrawn and become sullen, and this has become the very thing she hates. The world system teaches us that we have a right to look out for ourselves and fight to survive, while what you've taught us is that just the opposite is true.

"Living this way means giving up on my 'beguiling anticipations,' as you call them, that cloud my thoughts and emotions and that the world keeps throwing at us from every direction."

I agreed with Darryl and gave him and Mattie a handout done by Kay that shows the paradox of experiencing life in Christ. It summarizes that we die to live, lose to find and decrease to increase. We must surrender to be free, be broken to be whole, be empty to be full and be weak to be strong. We must receive to give, rest to have victory, work to rest and rest to work. And in doing so in marriage, we choose to love by sacrificing, or giving ourselves up, for the other. Life in the kingdom of God is mysteriously opposite than what the world and the flesh tell us. In other chapters, there will be examples of loving one's mate by this giving of one's self.

In his book, *The Marriage Builder*, Larry Crabb states,

The natural resistance to truly give ourselves to the other is rooted in our stubborn fear that if we really give, with no manipulative purpose, we will be shortchanged. Our needs will not be met. At best we will be disappointed; at worst we'll be destroyed. But God is faithful. We are to trust His perfect love to cast out fear, believing that as we give to our spouse in His name, He will supernaturally bless us with an awareness of His presence. And He will. But it may take time—perhaps even months—before we sense His work in us...Our job is to learn faithfulness and to press on in obedience, not giving in to discouragement or weariness...when a spouse becomes critical, drinks more heavily, or rejects efforts of ministry, we are to continue in our obedience, believing that our responsibility before God is to obey and to trust Him for the outcome (pp. 58-59).

These truths are definitely not of this world. Since Darryl had referred to the world's way of fighting, I wanted them to understand what I had been teaching them was about *arming themselves to fight with God's armor.* I wanted them to know a mysterious thing. And that is, *responding correctly* to the trial **is** God's armor and protection for a person! In the next chapter, I will elaborate on this.

A.W. Tozier, in his pamphlet, *The Old Cross and the New*, said that the old cross is different than the new one. Where the old one offered no compromise and brought life to us out of death, the "new and popular" cross says we can have both what the world offers and the cross of Christ at the same time. This lie can be put away only as we choose death to the precious old strategies by which we struggle to find life!

As I reflect on teaching the sobering reality of God's intention in the tests we face, I remember the congregation at the old church singing words that went like this,

On a hill far away stood an old rugged cross, the emblem of suffering and shame. To the old rugged cross, I will ever be true. Its shame and reproach gladly bear. I'll cherish the old rugged cross, until my trophies at last I lay down; I will cling to the old rugged cross and exchange it someday for a crown.

For many years of my life, I sang that hymn with no idea what those words meant. Honestly, if we knew, would we resist the truth of it?

Kay Ruff created this page, which illustrates the paradoxical nature of experiencing life in Christ here on this earth!

PARADOX

**Contradictory to What You'd Normally
Expect in Marriage, We Must**

Die to Live
Lose to Find
Decrease to Increase
Surrender to be Free
Be Broken to be Whole
Be Empty to be Full
Be Weak to be Strong
Receive to Give
Rest to Have Victory
Work to Rest
Rest to Work

**Sacrifice What is *Precious* [our fleshly strategies]
to Experience What is *Eternal***

*The joy of intimacy is experienced with God and in marriage
by acting on truth, receiving one's mate as he/she is
by sacrificing our fleshly life and strategies.*

Chapter 15

Arm Yourselves: This Is War!

> **On the Map:** This is a Jordan experience and will be repeated as we live in our new homeland of Canaan.

"Are you ready to declare war yet? Are you ready to arm yourselves and fight with different weapons when you face unfairness and resistance from each other—perhaps another attack of road rage—on your journey?"

My questions were unexpected. Perplexed, Darryl and Mattie turned to each other with blank stares as if they were wondering, "What in the world is she saying?" Then they expressed much curiosity in finding out what I meant.

When I asked Tony and Katrina the same question in their session, Tony's answer was, "We have received a lot of teaching, but I am ready to hear about this. It is just another of your surprises."

To explain, I told my couples the story of a preacher I'd heard about, who wanted to encourage and instruct church members, including husbands and wives who undoubtedly had experienced "road-rage"—sniper fire—from each other on their journey. In addition to wanting these individuals to love rather than hurt each other, he wanted them to know they shouldn't be afraid *if* others *did* bring inconveniences, accusations and unfairness against them. Furthermore, he told them they would *inherit a blessing if their response was correct* toward those who did do hurtful things.

To teach these truths, the preacher reminded them of who they were in Christ: chosen, holy, special. He said that because this was true, they should refrain from battling after old fleshly strategies and live in love and submission to one another. He gave instruction to all, specifically to husbands and wives, as to how this could be lived out with each other.

They were told they needed to be prepared so they wouldn't be surprised or blindsided when a trial came. The preacher explained that since sooner or later all would experience these tests, the listeners needed to know how to arm or gird themselves so they would be protected when they came under fire. Christ was called to suffer trials; we are called for the same purpose.

The preacher asked the people, "Who will harm you if you prove yourselves zealous for what is good?" Then he exhorted them to **arm themselves with** *the same purpose, or mind, as Christ.* They were to gird their *minds* for action. If these people were like me, they probably sat there in reflective silence wondering what he meant. This preacher was the Apostle Peter and the account is recorded in 1 Peter. They needed to learn how to fight with new weapons, put on new protective gear. And it involved a change of attitude, new thinking, a new mind-set.

Arm Yourselves: Capture the Terrorists

We have believed that our enemies, the terrorists who attack us on our journey, are *other people*, even our mates. It *feels* as though they are and we were always *told* they are. So, we wage war against our significant others; yet, the real terrorists that defeat us are *our thoughts*—our speculations and old myths about how we should protect ourselves and find fulfillment in our lives and relationships.

Our battles with our significant other can be silent manipulations or loud disagreements. Regardless, we must not war with each other with our old weapons. We are not to put any confidence in the old myths: that we must prove we are right, be in control, hold on to perceived entitlements and so on. These things fail us. Rather, we are to utilize God's armor and power weapons. This is a special-forces job and we must train ourselves in fighting this way in marriage. The weapons that win these wars are divinely powerful and they are for the purpose of pulling down the terrorist's strong fortress (2 Corinthians 10:3, Ephesians 6:12, Hebrews 12:11).

The walls of the terrorist's fortress in us are built of our myths and wrong thinking. When we utilize the weapon of Christ's attitude toward another, it tears down the fortress and we know God's protection in our experience, in our emotions. The way we engage in warfare with this weapon is *by taking all of our old thoughts captive to the obedience of Christ* (2 Corinthians 10:3–5).

Victory in our private wars with our mate is not won by *just* identifying our myths and reprogramming our heads with truth. It is not by *just* exercising faith and surrendering as we receive our trial. Although all of this is necessary, as we have already mentioned, another thing is needed, that is, *responding to our mate with the same purpose or mind as Christ.* The *mind* of Christ is His *attitude,* which is an illustration of His *obedience. This is His weapon against our foe,* especially in marriage!

"What?!" Tony said in his gravelly voice. "I don't understand."

"Our following Christ's obedience (His attitude) *is our weapon* against the terrorists, those myths and thoughts that defeat us as we relate with our spouse. This is the weapon that brings down and destroys the old strategies that prevent us from knowing God and His provision for us as we live with our marital partner. Boy, do we pride ourselves in our reason, our speculations and our guessing games when we fight with our significant other using the fleshly weapons! And it backfires on us. We war and still do not have what we need."

I leaned forward to make my point with Tony and Katrina. I said, "You must understand that allowing Christ's attitude to be *your* new attitude will not only be your armor for emotional protection, but *it is the very will of God for you, because His will is your being conformed to Christ's image, or His attitude.*

"This means each of you are to not only accept the other with their baggage, but you are to *respond to each other with the mind-set of Christ. This is the way you fight in marriage.* Responding in this way *is the obedience of the Christian life* in any situation. But your marriage relationship is the first setting in which you are to respond in this manner, because marriage is to be a living illustration of Christ's relationship with the church. This is when you find intimacy with God *and* each other. You will experience God's nurturing, His satisfying your neediness, His filling your emptiness, His protecting you emotionally."

Katrina asked in her terse voice, "What do you *mean*? What *is* the attitude you're talking about? Please *help* me to understand."

I said, "Christ's *attitude* toward others in all situations, *including His* response to trials, is that *image*, likeness or picture of who He is, and it is described in the Philippians 2:2–8. These verses describe what Christ's attitude of obedience "looked like." They also describe what *our* obedience to God is to be. After being told to consider others more important than ourselves, verses 5–8 describe what attitude we must have in doing this. We are told to *let* or allow this attitude be in us, which was also in Christ Jesus (Philippians 2:5 KJV). When we consistently do this as we let go of old myths, we 'take every thought captive to the obedience of Christ'." Surrendering old myths or hindrances lets, or allows, His attitude to be made manifest.

Following are the characteristics of His mind-set, which is to also be our mind-set.

- He knew who He was, but it was not an identity He could use to His own advantage.

- He became of no reputation, or emptied Himself of His rights as God, to be totally dependent on the Father.

- He took the attitude of a servant.

- He humbled Himself. (He did not defend or justify His position. He was always right but did not try to prove that He was. He was willing to appear wrong.)

- He became obedient to the death of the cross.

Christ Jesus gave up His right to exercise His authority as God and to prove He was right in order to allow Himself to be crucified. Since He knew who He was, He wasn't defensive. He didn't try to justify Himself or save Himself. And *if we know who we are* in Christ, we will experience Christ's empowering and sustaining life when we die to our own ways *with the same attitude—or attitude.*

He loved and served in response to the accusers, mockers and attackers in His life. *The human mind cannot comprehend this, and this is the reason Scripture tells us to no longer walk in the futility of our own minds.* This is sacrificial and what love is all about, and no one can find abundant life in marriage without it.

This is the crucial key to walking in the victory that is our inheritance in Christ. This mind-set of obedience is one characterized by humility and not trying to protect or promote our self-image or our own way. We do not have to because our worth is in Christ, not in our performance or others' acceptance. This is *an attitude* of the heart, in which we aren't self-protective when wrongly accused or misunderstood because we know Christ in us is our protection. This is true *repentance*—our turning around by *a change of our mind.*

Tony didn't seem like a laid-back teddy bear as he reacted to all of this. "I have always heard that if I am right and I know it, I should never give in. I think you're saying that even if I *am* right, I should not hold on to that. It will be hard, if Katrina withdraws from me and I am hurting, to trust God for my emotional protection, respond with a servant's attitude, esteeming her better than myself. It will feel like death!"

"Absolutely. But that is how true surrender is lived out. Sooner or later, your emotions will begin to line up," I replied. "It is often a sobering insight to become aware that being 'right' can be very wrong. If I am right and don't have love, I am as hollow as the resounding of a gong or the clanging of a cymbal (1 Corinthians 13:1). For example, I may be right to think we should invest our money a certain way, but I am wrong to lay a guilt trip on my spouse or demand that it be my way. Perhaps my way of loading the dishwasher is more efficient, but I am wrong when I criticize my spouse about not doing it my way.

"Would you rather be right or have peace and fulfillment as you live in your marriage? Do you want to nail Katrina for not telling you she will be late? You may be right, but you are left hollow like that resounding gong. No one has ever known fulfillment in marriage except by responding to one's mate in the way described. Jesus said that whoever will be first or greatest or leader will be the servant—that astounding paradox."

1 Peter 2: 19–23 says that our Christian calling by God is to patiently endure harsh treatment especially when we are right, just as

Christ suffered in this way, leaving an example for us as His followers. This is what finds favor with God. Even when He was reviled, His response was that He did not do the same in return. His submission to the Father and giving Himself up was lived out in this way.

Immediately following these comments, in the third chapter of 1 Peter we are told that wives and husbands are to likewise live with this kind of response toward each other. The wife's submission is lived out in holy and respectful behavior and the husband's is lived out as he gives honor to his wife and lives in an understanding way with her.

A transformation happens in us when we choose this new attitude and fight in marriage with new weapons (Romans 12:2). We are renewed in the spirit of our mind and we put on the new self that has been created in righteousness and holiness (Ephesians 4:22–24). We become a living sacrifice (Romans 12:1). We learn to know Christ by taking His attitude when we face the burdens or tests of life. If we are diligent and *continue in this to the end of our test*, we will experience the emotional rest, the joy and the fulfillment that are ours in Christ (Hebrews 3:8–15; 12:1–7, Colossians 1:22,23). We mature in Christ, are conformed to His image and find fulfillment within marriage at the same time. *All of this happens at the same time and in the same way!*

Jesus used a metaphor suitable to His day in describing His heart *attitude.* He said it was like that of oxen being harnessed into servitude by a wooden yoke so they could pull the weight of a burden. He said His *yoke* is easy and His *burden* is light. Jesus was saying that our having His attitude is an *easy* yoke with which we choose to allow ourselves to be harnessed. And the trial is a *light* burden—*far* lighter than the burden of our old strategies defeating us. He said, "Take My yoke upon you and learn from Me, for I am gentle and lowly in heart, and you will find rest for your souls" (Matthew 11: 29:30 NKJV).

In the past, sometimes I thought I had a right to claim the promises just because of who I was in Christ, or if I could conjure up enough belief, or if I did enough good works to please God. But the truth is, as long as I serve my old fleshly ways, I have no real privilege to partake of the promises of Christ. God has blessed me all along, but I have no real *rights* to enjoy my inheritance unless I am *being conformed to that likeness of Christ*, because my old laws and strategies block me from experiencing the good things God has already freely given me by His grace.

Receiving the trial and surrendering with the mind-set of Christ DOES NOT mean:

- Engaging in emotional dependency, manipulation or just "giving in" in marriage.

- A spouse should stay in a physically or emotionally violent relationship. It means to accept the abuse *as fact*, report it if appropriate, and respond with the *attitude* of Christ.

- We do not confront when someone is cheating or deceiving us. It *does* mean we *do* speak out, but *with the attitude of Christ, speaking the truth in love*.

- We do not express our likes or desires to our mate. We *do* express them with the *attitude* of Christ, being surrendered to whatever the outcome.

- We are to be doormats. Being a doormat is in our *thinking*. When we "please" to try to find acceptance as we live out of others' opinions, we become doormats. We can voluntarily serve others only when we know our worth in Christ.

- We stop caring. It means the realization that we can't "fix" things for others and must allow them to take responsibility for their choices and learn from natural consequences.

- Passivity or withdrawing from another. It *is* to know we can't control others or outcomes.

In one partner's choice to serve, submit and give him/herself up for the other, *that spouse's own neediness will be satisfied in Christ*. Knowing this enables one to stop trying to protect self and change the mate. This, in turn, interrupts defeating and repetitive interactions between them! It takes two to be in a power struggle. For example, when two are in a rope-pulling contest to see who can pull the other to his side, if one drops his end of the rope, it ends the struggle.

Darryl and Mattie

Turning to Mattie, I asked her if she could now see why I had waited to answer her question, which was, "What would surrender and trusting Christ look like in our relationship?"

She replied, "I think so. Even though we have surrendered, if you had told us *how it would look*, we would have tried to change our *behaviors* to line up, rather than our *attitudes*. Now I understand that it must be a change of our hearts."

Mattie was very quiet and reflective. She hooked her sun-streaked hair behind her ear. Her tell-tale right shoulder pushed forward and then relaxed. I noticed that her eyes were becoming red. "Wow," she said. "I want to say, 'But since I am not Christ, I can't do this,' but you have already blown away that excuse by preparing us with the knowledge of who we are in Christ and that it is by His life and indwelling power that we must respond. I have been so wrong. I have been "religious" and critical of Darryl when I didn't even know the truth myself."

Darryl, who used to pontificate, was cautious and his response was surprising. "I am stunned by everything you have taught us and it will take time to soak in," he said. "But I sense an excitement in me that I can't explain. I have never heard the Christian life or marriage explained like this. I believe I want to arm myself and do war with Christ's attitude."

"Congratulations! You have just been given your new protective armor and your new weapon—the truth of receiving Mattie with the attitude of Christ. Now arm yourselves with it and be prepared to fight! When you relate with each other in this way, what may *feel* like defeat will turn out to be life and you will possess every good thing in Christ. It is then that you will truly know Him—not just know *about* Him."

Darryl and Mattie were close to leaving their beguiling anticipations behind.

When Christ was on the cross, His response resulted in victory over Satan. Satan and his armies *are* defeated but today they try to defeat us by deception. While there is a place for rebuking the demons, our ultimate resistance to the devil, our armor of protection and the weapon that the powers of darkness cannot stand against *is our submission to God in receiving our circumstances with the attitude of Christ. This is when we "fight the good fight of faith."*

In my youth, during a winter service, the members in the country church stood quietly reflective. Our song leader, L. O. Butler, found a hymn in which the words supported the message of the sermon that had just concluded. Brother Revels announced, as he always did after he preached, "The doors of the church are open to receive anyone who is led to make a profession of faith. So, come now as we worship the Lord in song." I don't remember the sermon, but those words that now ring in my soul as I write are,

> Must I be carried to the skies on flowery beds of ease, While others fought to win the prize, and sailed through bloody seas? Sure I must fight if I would reign; Increase my courage Lord! I'll bear the toil, endure the pain, supported by thy Word.

I had no clue what these powerful words meant on that day years ago. But they go on to ask, "Are there no foes for me to face? Must I not stem the flood? Is this vile world a friend to grace, to help me on to God?" The song is titled, "Am I a Soldier of the Cross" and was written in 1724 by Isaac Watts. The one who wrote it knew the truth that we will reign in life if we fight the good fight of faith, supported by Christ and His truth.

The Journey leads to a New Highway: A toll road

As the traveling couples arrive in the new and unfamiliar land of their inheritance on the other side of the river, their journey leads to a new highway. The toll for traveling on the new road requires sacrifice of the self-life and putting on this attitude of Christ. Along the toll road, battles must be fought by this fight of faith. Strong and resistant people rarely enter this highway of holiness because the price is too high for them. It means surrendering pride and old ways when there are hurts and slights and opportunities to advance one's self in the marital relationship.

God resists the proud and gives grace to the humble. Roy Hession, in *Calvary Road,* says the thing in us that reacts so sharply to another's selfishness and pride is our *own* selfishness and pride that we are unwilling to sacrifice. *When we are sensitive and resentful, we are self-indulgent!* Hession asks, in effect, if we are willing, as Christ was, to be as a lamb shorn of what is due us and shorn of our reputation, without grudges and defensiveness. We must be emptied of ourselves on this highway so He can fill us.

For one to be at this place, time must be spent in intimate fellowship with God and in prayer. As we allow ourselves to be emptied, we should ask for His healing and for His Spirit to fill us. We must get to know God as our Father.

When we seek to journey in this place, our road is one of maturity and holiness, and it is a safe place to be. Scripture says of this highway, "No lion shall be there, nor shall any ravenous beast go up upon it..." (Isaiah 35:9 NKJV). Traveling this road is living in the kingdom of God and putting on Christ's righteousness where all we need and hunger for will be experienced (Matthew 6:33). Remember, this is a life process and it takes time.

When I am ready for the Lord to shape me or conform me into Christ's likeness in this way, in my relationship with my spouse, my responding out of emotion must give way to a focus on the truth of God's faithfulness to fill me and satisfy my neediness. I will lay down my old thoughts that things must be fair. I will risk looking wrong rather than trying to prove I am right to maintain my need of *Worth*. I will cease struggling to make my needs of *Security* and *Contentment* happen by speculations or "mind-reading" others' motives. I will cease trying to "fix" and direct, and know God has provided all I need. I will risk being vulnerable and not withdraw emotionally while trusting God to be the refuge of my soul. I will become weak in my own strength instead of striving to control outcomes.

Following is a summary of these old versus new attitudes.

ARM YOURSELF: THIS IS WAR

To fight the good fight of faith along a new highway is to:

Exchange old attitude *armor* for new attitude *armor* within marriage

EXCHANGE:

Old attitude *armor*	for	New attitude *armor*
❑ Demanding my way		❑ Having a servant's attitude
❑ Responding by FEEL		❑ FOCUSing on truth
❑ Pride		❑ Humility
❑ Fighting for fairness		❑ Accepting unfairness
❑ Manipulating to meet needs		❑ Relying God's provision
❑ Defensiveness		❑ Vulnerability
❑ Being strong		❑ Relinquishing strength in myself
❑ Proving you are right		❑ Willing to look wrong
❑ Struggling for security		❑ Waiting on God's provision
❑ Fighting by your "reason"		❑ Not relying on your own understanding
❑ Control		❑ Relinquishing control
❑ Avoiding/withdrawing		❑ Facing rejection while trusting God

Tony and Katrina

Katrina still struggled with her emotions and old beliefs. "Sometimes my head whirls with all of this new information. It's to face the fact that I might never have what I've longed for all my life and have hoped to find in a husband. However, I do believe in my head what you have taught us about Christ fulfilling us by whatever means He chooses."

She continued, "I feel this comforting warmth within me as I hear the truths you are teaching. But as I have said before, accepting a marital partner with their offensive ways is different than anything we have ever heard. I've never known anyone who lives this way."

Tony reasoned, "I relate to what Katrina said. Also, the concept of receiving Katrina with the attitude of Christ and seeking to please her when she rejects me or is rude to my family sounded so theological, but I am beginning to understand. I've thought a lot about all of this. Are you saying that our surrender and obedience to God is lived out in our attitudes of humility and sacrifice toward each other regardless of whether the other responds as they should? Are you saying *this is love*?"

I was elated. "Yes! Thank you! I couldn't have said it better," I replied. "Also, when you love in this way, you will refrain from accusing the other of being selfish even if they are. This is when, as it says in Ephesians 5:2, you walk in love, just as Christ has loved you and gave Himself up for you in an offering and sacrifice to God. This is also when you are putting on the new self, which is created in righteousness and holiness (when our *souls* are *being conformed* to match up to Christ in our *spirits*)."

Tony quickly said, "I have thought that I had hurts, anger and depression because of Katrina's attitudes toward me. From what you're saying, I am responsible for my *own* attitudes, and I have been experiencing the results of *my own way*. What's more, I will continue to if I don't have Christ's attitude toward her."

Katrina looked at Tony for the first time. "I also am hearing that. But I want to know what this kind of love will *look like* in our relationship," she said. I said that I would soon give some helpful examples of what it might look like.

Summarizing

I summarized for my couples what they had learned so far: "First, you discovered your myths and old strategies and compared them to your identity in Christ and God's truth of His sufficiency for you. But that was not enough.

"You then learned that you must pass through trials to bring you to a place of surrender and reliance on the Lord. Even though all of this is necessary to experience being complete and fulfilled in Christ in your marriage, it is not enough. In addition, you found you must have the correct response to your mate, which is the attitude of Christ and the will of God for you. I have summarized these concepts in the following manner:

Even though **all of the following are necessary** to experience being complete and fulfilled and have intimacy within marriage,

▲ It is NOT ENOUGH to just *know your myths and old beliefs.*

▲ It is NOT ENOUGH to just *know your identity* in Christ!

▲ It is NOT ENOUGH to just *replace old beliefs with new ones.*

▲ It is NOT ENOUGH to just *pass through trials.*

▲ It is NOT ENOUGH to *surrender in the face of trials.*

Your experience of Christ satisfying your needs
for fulfillment and intimacy as you live with your mate:

Only Happens

when you face trials and resistance
as well as ordinary times in marriage

with the

Correct Response

The attitude of Christ—that paradox
This is when we are being conformed to His image,
which is His will for us

It is important to remember that:

- What we were originally attracted to in our mate can be the source of frustrations later.

- We select the partner who resists us and has strategies that frustrate and pain us in the very areas where we are most needy.

- These hurts and frustrations are opportunities for us to trust Christ to satisfy our needs as we surrender and respond with His attitude.

- As that happens, we learn to fight with new weapons. This is when we are being conformed to Christ's image, which is the will of God for us.

- This is when we walk after the Spirit with the life of Christ flowing out. We bear His fruit and experience fulfillment and enjoy the good things God had provided in Christ as we live within marriage.

Following is a visual illustration of what happens in us when we live out the truth.

A New Creation Walking After the Spirit: Spirit, Soul and Body

As a regenerated believer begins to understand the truth of the indwelling Christ and his/her freedom from the power of sin, then chooses to allow the "testings" of life to work in him/her so that reliance on the flesh is broken and those dependencies are transferred to Christ, we see an individual who is "Walking After the Spirit." The individual is "ceasing from his own works" and abiding in Christ. We could say that the "chaff" is being removed, the light is not being placed under the "bushel," the "childish things" are being put away, and so on. When this happens, Christ's life flows out like rivers of living water and "appears" through us! The diagram below might be a helpful aid in understanding this truth.

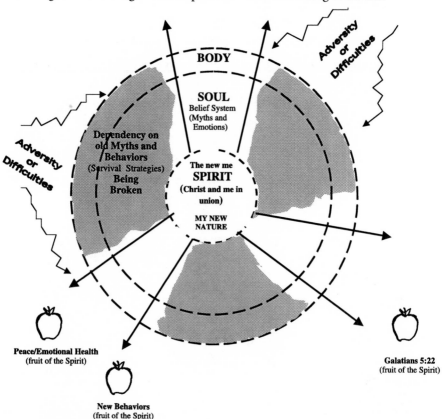

Dependency on flesh is being "broken" and Christ's life is flowing out

Chapter 16

A Toll Road: What Will It Look Like?

> **On the Map:** In Canaan, on the new highway.

Since Darryl and Mattie, as well as Tony and Katrina, were getting prepared to take a turn onto a new and unfamiliar toll road, they were eager to know what all of this would look like in their marital relationships.

The couples had a good foundation established for learning to live out of truth in a practical way. Without this basis, they would continue to struggle in their own efforts to change behaviors and emotions with the root problems never being solved. Old damaging patterns would resurface. So, this was the right time to illustrate how relating differently might look and even feel.

We have seen there are different styles of living life in relationships. Different varieties of flesh were formed to protect us from failure and rejection and to meet needs of *Contentment, Security* and *Worth*. We tend to hold on to these protections and methods with our lives, and *although it may be unconscious to us, whatever we need to let go of emotionally is what we fear we can't live without.*

In helping them see what taking a new road and living with new attitudes might look like, I first illustrated some automatic thoughts or fears they could have as they faced the choice to relinquish old patterns. *Of course, this thinking does not represent truth, and they will have to choose to walk right straight through these fears, believing God's truth.*

In Darryl and Mattie's counseling session, I said to Darryl, "You might think, 'If I surrender my "right" to withdraw into my safe place, and come out and get involved with the family, I might be humiliated or rejected if I fail.'"

In a strange way, Darryl's withdrawing or distancing from Mattie perpetuated her demands and her pursuit. And her pursuit made him feel important. *Mattie, and others who emotionally pursue, must stop trying to connect and make the other show love. Then she must refrain from reconnecting in the same old ways if the emotional distancer stops withdrawing!* This is extremely important, otherwise the same old patterns will resurface.

Mattie might fear that she would feel loneliness forever and there would never be any chance of finding validation in marriage if she relinquished her strategies and her emotional pursuit of Darryl and accepted his withdrawing and withholding ways.

I told Tony and Katrina his fear might be, "If I let go of pursuing Katrina, demanding respect and sex from her, I could feel I'm not a real man. And I might never have that sense of connectedness I so desire."

"Katrina, you might tend to believe, 'If I draw boundaries between myself and my children, it would mean I am giving up the only way I know to try to find love and validation. I might be hurt if I quit distancing into my safe place and became vulnerable with Tony,'" I said.

I explained to Latoya that she could think: "If I surrender dependency on being super-responsible and Joe's care-taker, we could be left homeless or our children wouldn't turn out right. Maybe I would be giving up my ways of feeling significant."

Yet another person might be afraid that if he let go of his defenses, he would be seen as weak and would be taken advantage of.

We will be out of our comfort zone and it will feel "risky." Of course, it is not a risk at all to those in Christ. Dr. Larry Crabb, in his book, *The Marriage Builder*, compares this "risk taking" in marriage to jumping off a cliff. It is as if we are standing on a cliff that represents our "security," and to jump off would mean we risk being destroyed by the rocks of rejection or failure at the bottom. Remember, this concept was included in the prayer of surrender. However, it is when we jump that our faith in Christ's protection for us is exercised. This doesn't mean that we won't *feel* fear or pain while we are waiting for the experience of the Lord's sufficiency. But our experience of His provision will come—we may have to just wait it out a little while.

When we are brought to a point of frustration in a time of difficulty with our mate, we can choose to yield up our old way. Nancy Groom, in her book, *Married Without Masks*, also calls this "cliff-jumping," which means we give up the "security" of trying to make our partners be more loving. *It is always false security that we resist giving up.* But loving our spouse is the willingness to trust Christ and drop our guardedness, control and demands that he or she change.

Tony and Katrina

Clarifying what the toll road would look like for Tony, I said, "If you are going to love Katrina and respond with Christ's attitude, you must be willing to be rejected. You must quit your pursuit, which would feel threatening. It will feel risky, but when you are focused on the truths you have learned, your identity in Christ and His faithfulness to you, you can choose *not* to receive Katrina's distancing as a message about your lack of value. You will be secure in knowing that you have been made adequate and complete in Christ. Then you can let go of your demands that Katrina do everything a certain way in order for you to feel loved and validated as a man. And you can respond in humility and submission."

I turned to Katrina, "This, of course, does not mean that it is okay for you to reject Tony! But we are facing situations that *might happen.* As for you, one of your familiar patterns is to feel you do not measure up and to look for rejection in Tony's behaviors. You distance into your "safe" place that isn't safe at all, but it seems better than what you've feared. You must move out into a place of continuously reminding yourself that in Christ there is emotional safety and your fulfillment and worth will never be found in another's attention and responses. You have tried to get sympathy and "love" by self-pity. It hasn't worked. You two "hook" each other by your old ways and keep the cycle of defeat on going.

You need to "unhook" and choose to be available to Tony and find ways of serving him in love."

Katrina responded, "I've felt if Tony wasn't pleased or if he put me down, that confirmed to me that I do not deserve love or that I am a failure. You're saying I'll have to remember that my identity is not based in shame from my past or in what Tony may think but in the righteous life of Christ in me. I am beginning to understand my identity is in who God has made me as a new creation. I will have to constantly recall that the Lord will fill me as I surrender the belief that my behavior must be perfect for me to be acceptable. I need to remind myself that I have been made accepted in Christ. I have to remember that Tony is just reacting to me out of his own issues. But it won't be easy to remember these things."

"No, it isn't easy to continue to set your focus on truth. But remember, it is that fight of faith we discussed. You will experience God's goodness in ways you have never imagined," I said.

Latoya

When Latoya asked what putting on new attitudes might be like for her in relation to Joe, I replied, "When you find yourself holding on stronger to an old pattern, know you are being controlled by a fear. An example is your having to stay in charge to feel secure. You will need to change your thinking and remember that your security in every area is in the Lord. *You must understand that you do not have the power in yourself to control Joe, times and circumstances.* You must realize that Joe, as each of us, is responsible for himself. You can accept Joe and often choose to do things he suggests, even if "your reason tells you that your way is the best way."

It is important to remember that controlling behavior is not just dominant behavior. It can reflect the sweet, dependent person who appeases and lives as an extension of what the spouse, or others, think. That person feels inadequate and fears that if others see him make mistakes, they will reject him. A "pleaser" often manipulates others so that he doesn't have to make decisions and have to risk rejection if the outcome is undesirable. He will ask, "Do you want me to do so and so?" *Whether the answer is yes or no, it makes the other person is the culprit.* When they do this, they put the responsibility on the other person so they won't have to be blamed. They can blame the other! "Pleasing," like any type of control, is idolatry because others' responses become one's God.

This individual must remember his identity and worth are in Christ only, choose to draw boundaries by saying 'no' when appropriate, make decisions and refrain from manipulating by people-pleasing behaviors. He must risk looking wrong and being rejected.

What It Looks Like

When we yield up our controlling strategies to walk in truth, this **IS** to:

1. *Detach* from the past and from being caught in defeating relational patterns.
2. *Draw boundaries.*
3. *Realize we cannot control others* to give us what we need.

Following are some examples of what surrender to God and a change of attitude might look like in various individuals. An individual may have a combination of these strategies. Remember that one's *focus* is never to be on trying to "deal with" or "die to" these fleshly strategies. It must be on the truth of Christ's sufficiency and on having the Philippians 2:5–8 mind-set.

■ The *"blamer"* must accept his or her share of the blame and/or just *risk looking wrong*, knowing Christ is his justifier and emotional protection.

■ The *abuser* might admit his fear of emotional abandonment or weakness and acknowledge Christ's sufficiency as he *humbles himself*, relinquishes defensiveness and control, learns to listen and does acts of gentle kindness.

■ The *demanding* **selfish person** would have to *know that love is giving, not getting or being "catered to."* He would choose to stop interpreting every action as a rejection and learn to serve and build up his mate in the truth, demanding nothing in return.

■ The *co-dependent "people-pleaser" who manipulates* would have to *risk the family and herself looking bad* as she stops trying to "fix" and "rescue" and "orchestrate." She must stop trying to validate her worth by her service to others. She must quit her false submission and compliance that comes from fear of rejection. She must cease her emotional dependency by pursuing *connectedness*. She must refrain from thinking and saying, "I can't do anything to please you. You don't appreciate all I've done." She must remind herself that her completeness and approval will be found in Christ, not another person.

■ The *uninvolved emotional distancer* would "risk" getting emotionally involved, learn to listen, have the attitude of a servant and choose to take more responsibility. He might have *to risk "failure" and criticism* while knowing his adequacy, security and peace is to be found in Christ.

■ The *dependent "pleaser"* who avoids decisions and fears rejection will "risk" thinking about what he wants and *decide to do that thing without having to have his mate's help* in decision-making. He must know he can do all things he needs to do through Christ, who also has made him accepted. He needs to remember that as he loves God and chooses to walk in truth, God will work *all* things (even one's "failures") together for the person's good and for God's glory.

■ Other *emotionally dependent people* often manipulate with self-pity. When things don't go their way they pout, and when they are asked if something is wrong, they say "no." These people must acknowledge their self-centered ways and relinquish dependency on the myth that love means being catered to or getting their way. They must choose to risk the pain of things not going their way and realize that emotional needs are met only in Christ as they take on His mind-set.

■ The *pursuing* or *argumentative* spouse will have to *lose the pride* of having to "be right," and quit trying to prove he/she is right or best— while looking wrong. This person as the others, must allow himself to be humbled and know God will exalt him in due time.

■ The *perfectionistic, controlling spouse* will have to let go of having to have "all his ducks in a row" and *"risk" losing his security being in his having order* and in another's acceptance. He must know the Lord is his security and has made him accepted.

■ The spouse whose opinion *"has to be heard"* and who has to prove he knows more than the other or who needs to "go them one better," topping what the other says to validate his significance will need to risk not telling his stories for a while, and *practice listening skills* rather than interrupting, talking over and answering for the other. He must remind himself the Lord has made him of worth and abide in that fact.

■ The *super responsible controller* must *quit rescuing his mate* from irresponsibility by doing it all, covering for him and bailing him out and allow the mate to experience the consequences of the irresponsible behavior. This person (as all who begin change) must let the partner know of his support, love and acceptance. He must trust God for whatever outcome. He must know that God will work things together for good for him because he loves God and is called according to His purpose. He must realize the end result may not be what he had envisioned.

■ The one with a *victim mind-set* must catch himself when he verbalizes or thinks how he has been unfairly treated. He, as the others here, must *quit kicking against unfairness* and trying to get another to change. He must forgive and remember that healing and emotional protection is to be found only in the Lord. He must remember his worth in Christ and choose to become emotionally available to his mate. If there is physical abuse, he will not receive it. He will report it and understand that he is not to blame for the abuse. He will say "no" to inappropriate behaviors. He will leave for a safe place if there is abuse.

Did you find that you had some of these defeating patterns? Did you get ideas of how you could begin to think differently as you relate? It is extremely important to know that this new thinking and behaving must be practiced in *all* of one's relationships in order for change and fulfillment to come. An attitude of humility and unselfish giving and considering your mate to be better than yourself must accompany all of these changes.

U-turns Encouraged

Since the word *repentance* means to turn around and go in the opposite direction by a *change of mind* (or attitude), these changes bring a kind of "U-turn" on our journey as we face oppositions and hindrances as well as ordinary circumstances. This is a change in our *soul*, which is also referred to as a change of *heart* or our *keeping our heart* with diligence.

We must remember that any temporary satisfaction we got from our old ways was never lasting. Waiting until we are in the heat of conflict and arguments to focus on truth is simply too late. Our decision to trust Christ while changing our thinking must be an ongoing conscious choice from the time we get up in the morning until the time we go to bed at night. And it takes practice. Otherwise we will be blindsided by our emotions when someone questions us, slights us or hinders us.

Some important words: *Since we are so addicted to the old strategies (they are our "fix"), there may be withdrawal symptoms when we relinquish dependency on the old ways! You might feel as if you will lose the relationship. Also, it is predictable that when one spouse begins to change, it is not only unfamiliar territory to that spouse, but it can feel threatening to the other as well! The other mate will try (perhaps unconsciously) to pull back the spouse who made the changes, into old familiar ways of relating. For example, when you quit your pursuit for emotional connectedness, your partner may begin pursuing you! However, when you resist going back to the old strategies, he may become angry and threatening. It will take constant choices to trust God and not to be pulled back into your old ways—into operating from old myths about getting needs met and into the old behaviors of pursuing or distancing.*

Your mate may not like your old ways, but they are predictable and your reactions to him are familiar. The point is for you not to be surprised if your mate even strengthens his old patterns to an uncomfortable intensity when you begin to change.

Since this is a lifetime process, as time passes it will become more and more automatic to shift our focus to "things above" or to truths that are spiritually higher than our old ways. We must also have support from the body of Christ, people who can encourage and support us in truth on an ongoing basis. It is vital to study and recall truth from written pages that we can keep before our eyes and spend time listening to God. We must remember also that head knowledge becomes heart knowledge with each step we take in faith.

The illustrations in this chapter helped our couples to understand how giving themselves for the other and putting on the mind of Christ might look and feel in their relationships. But they all continued to wonder how to handle old emotions. Defeating emotions are so powerful, and everyone wanted to know the answer to a question Mattie had asked earlier, "But, what do I do with my emotions? How do I choose to set my mind on the truth when I have all of these powerful *feelings* in the way?" I will address these questions in the next chapter.

Proofs of Change

I explained to my counselees that certain evidences develop in a person when he has come to this place of surrender and truly desires to put on the attitude of Christ in his relationships. This is the brokenness of which we have spoken. I have included a "Proofs of Brokenness and the Attitude of Christ" checklist that has been helpful to almost everyone I have counseled.

Proofs of Brokenness and the Attitude of Christ

1. All presumed "rights," "privileges," and "entitlements" surrendered.

2. Willing to be rejected.

3. Transparent: willing to share weaknesses.

4. Not having to prove you are right.

5. Recognizing inadequacy in old strategies.

6. Trusting in Christ's adequacy, His strength.

7. Obedience out of a love motive because you want to, not because you have to.

8. Trusting that God is your refuge, even with external turmoil.

9. Willing for the Lord to fulfill you, rather than demanding fulfillment from your mate or your performance.

10. Willing to serve and build up your mate, esteeming him/her better than yourself.

11. Willing to fail or appear a failure.

12. A readiness to let others receive credit.

13. Willing to be humbled; to receive your mate with his/her imperfections.

14. Willing to receive your trial as God's instrument to perfect you.

15. Willing to not be defensive or to justify yourself.

16. Willing not to speculate or "mind read" motives.

17. Relinquishing control, fixing and directing.

18. Willing to be misunderstood.

19. Willing to become "of no reputation" (KJV).

Adapted from material developed by Grace Ministries International by permission.

Write out what it would look like to respond sacrificially,
with the mind of Christ, to your mate's old strategies and
imperfections. What would you be doing differently?

1. Definitely give up my rights –
to be treated the way I think I
should be treated.

2. Willing to be rejected – hard one
for me. BIG FEAR

3. Trust God's adequacy – His strength

4. Trust God to fulfill my needs,
emotional, financial – not Glenn.

5. Receive trials as God's instrument
to perfect me

6. Not speculate or mind read
motives!

Chapter 17

Ready, Set, Go! "But What About My *Emotions?*"

> **On the Map:** Crossing Jordan and/or in Canaan.

Tony wore his red shirt with the company logo. He leaned back. He looked toward the ceiling and his face became flushed. With his elbow resting on the arm of my sofa, he shielded his quivering mouth with his hand.

He said, "I desire to live this life in Christ but how can I get past my *emotions?* I have come to the conclusion they have controlled me all my life, especially in my relationship with Katrina. I do believe what you have told us is truth, but I have lived all my adult life with the expectation that I should get what I need emotionally from my wife. What do I do with the devastating *feelings* of disappointment?"

I emphasized that as Tony began to walk with his focus on listening to God, learning the truth of his identity in Christ, and on the Lord's faithfulness to provide emotionally while choosing to respond with the correct attitude, *over time* his emotions *would* begin to change. *Peace would come.*

Walking in truth is a *choice* we make; it is not based on emotions. Emotions aren't bad, but they cannot be relied on. Damaging emotions do not represent truth. We must not make decisions based on them. If we do, we wind up being controlled by them. Every day, we make conscious, intentional decisions to do things that we do not *feel* like doing. We make these choices in our jobs and at home. For example, we may not *feel* like getting up in the morning, but we do it and eventually our *feelings* line up. In the beginning, we may agonize while we choose to walk in truth. If we persevere, however, sooner or later joy and contentment will replace the old feelings.

Often, hurting individuals will come to counseling and tell me they have been told by a friend to "just get over it!" and to disregard their emotions. Of course, we should not deny our emotions. Denying *or* stuffing feelings *leads* to problems. In Scripture, we can see that Jesus Himself had many different emotions. ***But Christ's emotions were not damaging or defeating because they did not result from believing myths or lies.*** Having emotions is a part of how we are made as God's creations. Too often, though, we have been programmed to rely on emotions to guide us or be indicators of truth.

Some people by personality are more sensitive and feelings oriented while others seem to naturally be more objective. Yet, problems arise when we become *captive* to our emotions and they control us or when we begin to *rely on* our feelings to guide us in our lives. Many people have allowed their emotions to control them since childhood. These feeling have become familiar and automatic habits.

Damaging emotions may have become habitual if they have evoked a payoff from others or if they have been continually reinforced in some way in a person's life. If that is the case, this is a person who is ruled by how he feels. If an individual tries to change emotions simply by positive thinking or by ignoring them, he will fail in the attempt because the *beliefs behind the feelings* must be changed first.

As counselors, we do want to empathize with others, but *we do not want to validate defeating emotions* because we will be reinforcing the lies or myths *behind* the emotions. It is uncanny how often we validate a person's feelings and then try to teach them truth at the same time! I have had counselees say they believe truth but are still controlled by anxiety in certain areas. This person may believe a lot of truth, but he doesn't believe truth about God, himself and his presumed entitlements in relation to those areas that evoke the anxiety.

*It is very important to understand that **our circumstances and other people do not cause our damaging emotion;** rather, it is **what we believe about ourselves and how we are to stay safe and get needs met in the context of situations that causes the emotions.*** We have begun to see the validity of this statement as we have progressed through the book.

For example, imagine you and another person sitting in a room talking. Suddenly, a third person you both know angrily bursts through the door and starts accusing and demeaning each of you, pointing out your failures and threatening you. You may be very upset and start speculating about why and be depressed for days. The other person's response is to blow it off and not be affected by it for long. Each of you responds differently because of what you *believe about yourself in the situation.*

Emotions are the fruit of our beliefs—good *or* bad. We have been programmed by the world and our families to believe that circumstances or others **make us** angry, sad, hurt and so on, that others *are responsible* if we are or are not emotionally okay. This is a great deception.

Following is an illustration of the process of how a hurtful circumstance or an activating event filters through our belief system, which, in turn, evokes certain thoughts and emotions, and then produces certain actions or behaviors. I shared this with our couples, because it is often easier to comprehend a concept through a visual picture.

This illustration is based on what has been called the

$$A + B = C > D > E \text{ concept}$$

A Here, a **fearful circumstance, an insult, unfairness, an inconvenience or other event** enters your life.

+

$$B \quad = \quad C \quad >> \quad D \quad >> \quad E$$

Belief System	**Thoughts**	**Emotions**	**Actions**
(truth or error)	*(thinking process)*	*(feelings)*	*(behaviors, strategies)*

In order to change your thoughts, emotions and actions, your *beliefs* about yourself as related to your circumstances must change first. ***What lies or myths do you believe* that cause your emotions to be out of control and result in your continually feeling rejected, hurt angry, fearful, depressed, discouraged, depressed and so on?**

If you feel hurt and angry because you have been overlooked, not appreciated, insulted, treated unjustly—or if you feel fearful—*investigate what your lies or myths are behind these feelings. **Deceptive beliefs are behind all of our damaging emotions.*** Many of these false beliefs were listed on the charts entitled, "Myths vs Truth" and "Myths of Marriage."

In life, it is normal to experience anger, pain, disappointments and grief. But when our emotions begin to control us and defeat us in a certain area, we believe a lie related to that area of life. Believing the truth sets us free from these tormentors!

Scripture tells us that we are to be *transformed* by the *renewing of our minds*—**not** by changing emotions or behaviors. We must repack our bags with truth.

Ready, set (your mind), go!

You must practice this new life of *actively setting your mind* on the truth in *every situation* so you will be prepared when you face difficulty. Nevertheless, you will sometimes revert to being controlled by your feelings. In Gethsemane, Jesus agonized and struggled but KNEW the Father's faithfulness and was not going to rely on these feelings to deter Him from the cross.

Tony was struggling as I said to him, "Sometimes emotions cause us to believe that we can't endure our situation any longer. But the truth is that Christ can, and we can do all things *through Christ's working* through us. As you walk surrendered and setting your mind on truth, after a while you will experience the power and joy that was up ahead of you while you were running the race. You will win the prize!"

Tony's cynical response was that this seemed as if it would be living in the supernatural. "Yes! That is exactly what it is. It is living in God's kingdom. Stone and Smith, in *The Rest of the Gospel,* call it "living above the line" in the eternal realm," I said.

Suddenly Katrina's foot stopped jiggling. She said, "You know, I am realizing that I never *thought;* I just *did!* I reacted on what I felt. It will be a hard choice to focus on setting my thoughts on truth."

In Mattie's and Darryl's counseling session, Mattie wrestled with letting go of the belief that husbands and wives should "work-through, deal with and share" their hurt feelings in order to have intimacy. *I reminded her that when the focus is on validating hurt emotions, the false beliefs behind the emotions are reinforced.* Because these efforts are merely fleshly attempts to satisfy neediness, defeating patterns continue.

Mattie asked if I could give a practical illustration of the process someone had gone through while setting their mind. She said, "If I could hear how another person has handled emotions while trusting God in a situation, it would be helpful."

I was enthusiastic to let them read out loud Kay's written testimony of how she learned to "set her mind" in a simple, yet emotionally difficult, circumstance. This is one of her more practical illustrations of how she experienced the Lord's faithfulness in her relationship with her husband, Don.

Kay's "Tomato Testimony"

Standing in my kitchen early one morning, eager to get started on my long list of "to dos" meticulously mapped out to the very minute it would take to accomplish each one...my husband passes through on the run with a hug and kiss and a statement that would come very close to launching me into the "twilight zone"! "Honey, would you please water my tomato plants? I'm running late this morning and I'd really appreciate it! Bye!" You see, Don had a whole ARMY of tomato plants, all lined up in neat little rows and standing at attention. And I don't even like tomatoes.

I put on my smile, but inside there was war! I did not know that this moment was going to be a significant change point in my life...when I actually began to put into practice all that was simply information to me so far.

This was the process of beliefs, thoughts and emotions *[remember A + B = C>D>E ?]* that raced through me...

BOOM!
BOOM!
BOOM!

MY FALSE BELIEFS...

- I must be in control to **be secure.**
- I must perform perfectly to know I am **of worth.**
- I can't tolerate differences, hindrances, interruptions (for then I would be out of control, my performance would be inadequate and I would be of **no value!**).

MY THOUGHTS...

- He has no right to ask me to do that!
- He is just getting in my way!
- I don't have to do this!
- I don't want to do this!
- He can go jump in the lake!
- He makes me so mad!
- My whole day is ruined!
- I don't know why God doesn't change him!
- I don't even like tomatoes!

MY EMOTIONS...

- Anger
- Used
- Cheated out of my rights
- Helpless
- Depressed
- Hopeless

But, somehow I recalled some of the information that I knew. It went something like this:

THE TRUTH...

- My worth and value are not dependent on my performance (but on who I am in Christ)!
- I am angry! That's all right!
- This is not **my** life—anymore!
- Christ desires to express **His life** through me in this circumstance!
- I am a new person in Christ and I *want* to let **Him** live **His life** through me.
- I can choose to welcome this situation as an opportunity for Christ to minister to my husband.
- I can trust God to bring my emotions down to line up with truth.
- My whole day is *not* ruined.
- My husband is *not* my *enemy.*

At the onset, before I was bogged down in emotional wallowing and *thinking things to death,* I decided to offer myself as a living sacrifice to *God,* to let Christ live **His life** through me to minister to Don by watering his tomatoes. I didn't **"feel"** like it, but I wanted to walk by truth this time...so out the door I went, depending on Christ to water tomatoes through me...and He did. *Nothing is impossible with God.* I began to focus on the truths He was showing me, and in thirty minutes my spaced-out emotions began to subside and line up with the truth...and I actually began to experience **rest** as only He can give.

Before, I was a Christian trying desperately *to get love* and value in **MY life** (my fleshly way), and now I was seeing that God wanted me to understand how to *live from love*...by allowing Christ to live **His LIFE** through me to minister to others, *beginning with my spouse!*

Because our needs are met in Christ and we are totally and completely loved and accepted by Him, we are free to regard marriage not as a place to fill our needs but as a unique opportunity to help another become aware of God's love and purposes. We do this by letting Christ live His resurrection LIFE through us. When we have this attitude, God *may* choose to meet some of our needs through our mate, but we are not promised this will happen or that we are entitled to it.

This is our goal. But so much of the time, we desire that our spouses minister to us...and there is much pain when they fail to respond. Remember what God has said about you. He says you are a winner. You have the victory. **Victory is a gift. Victory is a person—Christ. It is not obtained or experienced by effort,** but by **receiving** Christ's work on our behalf, by **believing** the truth and by **ceasing** from our own fleshly works. This is illustrated by the "5 R's" listed below:

"The 5 R's" of Setting / Renewing My Mind

R **Recognize** a thought—that it is not Truth.

R **Refuse** to accept it or act on it.

R **Reckon** (count it as fact) that I am dead to sin and alive to God and all His promises are sure for me.

R **"Risk"** acting on what I know to be Truth.

R **Rest** When I experience the Lord's rest, I am assured that I am in Christ and He is in me by God's doing...I am safe, valued and He is taking care of the situation.

My goal now is to refuse to be controlled by what I see, think, or feel, but by what I know...Truth. I now understand that:

1) Our Christian work or service is our taking thoughts captive to the obedience of Christ.

2) We are to work out our own salvation...to "mine" or "work " what God has *already given us* out into to the open where it appears! (Philippians 2:12).

3) We are to practice these "good works" of obedience so that our senses will be exercised to discern good from evil (Hebrews 5:13).

Some Scriptures I must remember about "setting my mind":

- Romans 5: 8–10   I am **saved by His LIFE!**

- Romans 12:1   I am to present myself as a living sacrifice.

- Romans 8:5–6   If my mind is set on living the fleshly way, a walking death.

- 2 Corinthians 10:5 I must take every thought captive to the obedience of Christ.

- Colossians 3:2   I am to set my mind on things above.

- Ephesians 6:12–13a Setting my mind is WAR.

- Philippians 4:8   I must let my mind dwell on these things that are above my ways).

- 2 Timothy 1:7   God has given me *a spirit of* power, love and *a sound mind.*

- Romans 12:2   I am to be transformed *by* the renewing of *my* mind.

I'VE EVEN LEARNED TO LIKE TOMATOES NOW…a little.

Darryl responded, "Hearing that was very helpful, but choosing is difficult sometimes. And I don't know how to say this, but it is something we touched on earlier in our counseling. It relates to another area. It is the problem I have had in the past with lust and fanaticizing and the emotional highs that go with it, you know. Mattie has been hurt by it and has felt rejected by me. Often, it has felt as if I don't have any power to set my mind on truth where this is concerned."

"Darryl, I know others with the same problem who have found victory by understanding the truths you have learned and by continually choosing to 'take every thought captive to the obedience of Christ, casting down imaginations and every high thing that would exalt itself against the knowledge of God.' It will be a continual choice and, in the beginning, the choice will not come easy. In the beginning, the fantasy is an emotional escape from uncomfortable situations and a substitute for intimacy. Sometimes, it becomes addictive.

"I have known individuals who found freedom from this addiction by keeping Scripture in front of them continually. One individual kept a small booklet of relevant Scriptures in a shirt pocket so that when a temptation presented itself, there could be an *immediate choice* to refocus and set his mind on truth. God has already provided victory for you in Christ. Being tempted is not sin. Jesus was tempted. He felt the tugging to be drawn away but He did not succumb. He counteracted it with the Word. Darryl, you will be at war, in a fight of faith. And your weapon is setting your mind on truth."

I continued. "Darryl, your motive is to be setting your mind on loving God and giving yourself up for Mattie, and 'love never fails.' The choice is often hard, but remember, Christ is faithful to do it as you pursue knowing Him. This is to walk after the Spirit, and Galatians 5:16 says when we do so, we won't fulfill the desires of the flesh. This is true regardless of whether the problem is sexual temptation, anger, a critical tongue, or any other fleshly behavior. As I have said before, there may be occasions of falling down, but since you already have the victory in Christ, you can get back up and continue."

During this part of Darryl and Mattie's session, in a flash and from out of nowhere I heard the congregation at the country church softly singing the hymn, "Turn Your Eyes Upon Jesus," written in 1922 by Helen Lemmel. Its encouraging words reminded me that "the things of the earth will grow strangely dim" when our eyes are set on Christ and His grace.

I suddenly understood the truth of the words of the song as I quoted them to Darryl. Did the saints at the old white church that still stands on the open rise know the truth of which they were singing? Did they know back then that by setting one's mind on knowing God they would walk in the victory won by Jesus and freely given by God's grace?

These truths often seem so ethereal that we wonder how we can possibly walk them out in our personal situations. It has been extremely helpful to many of my counselees to use a table called, "Setting the Mind," to identify in writing hurtful or frustrating circumstances in marriage and then track their thoughts, emotions, myths and old behaviors across the table, ending with identifying new beliefs. It is especially useful to people who have been controlled by their emotions. This exercise can be tremendously helpful to exchange new thinking for old and to live out of truth daily. This table follows and is provided so that you can actively set your mind on truth.

The travelers take a turn on to a new highway and enter unfamiliar territory. This new road is where they learn to live setting their minds on truth. They can have assurance as they go because staying on this highway provides God's protection for them as they travel.

As the couples journey in this new land, they must leave the past in the past so they will not be controlled by it. However, each individual will need to forgive any past debts and leave past loyalties, before they can move ahead. We will address the concepts of forgiveness in the next chapter.

Renewing the Mind: Identifying Hurtful situations, Emotions, Thoughts, Myths, Old behaviors and Truth / New beliefs

Hurtful Situation	Emotions (Feeling words)	Thoughts	Myths (Old beliefs)	Old Behavior	New Belief/ Truth
Example: spouse is critical, withdraws from me	hurt, angry, rejected	I am not good enough, but I deserve better	I must be perfect to be loved and accepted	pout, withdraw, criticize, try harder	I have been made perfect, accepted and complete in Christ
infidelity	"	"	"	"	"

Entering unfamiliar territory:

My daily choosing to surrender
reliance on myths while

setting my mind on truth

and

putting on Christ's attitude while
trusting Him to be in charge of the outcome

and

not trusting my emotions

will bring

my experience of *Christ*
meeting my needs as I relate with my mate (or others)!

Part Four

At Home in a New Land

Chapter 18

New Loyalties in a New Land: Forgiving, Leaving and Cleaving

> **On the Map:** In Canaan. Learning to leave the past behind in their relationships.

I couldn't read their faces when Tony and Katrina arrived for their Thursday session. I had learned not to even try. They both seemed solemn.

During their weeks of counseling, they had alternated among curiosity, resistance and acceptance of the truth. Remember, although they had not been ready to surrender, they said they wanted to continue counseling.

I asked what was going on.

Tony replied, "We have something to tell you, Anne."

Katrina said, "After last week's session, both of us were convinced that we needed to be committed to what you have been teaching us. So, we decided to take Saturday just to be together and discuss our relationship and everything we'd learned."

Tony's muddy boots let me know he had been inspecting his high-rise construction downtown. He leaned forward. He propped his elbows on his knees and leaned his chin on interlocked fingers. Tears ran down from under his glasses. He said, "I have been so tired, so fatigued, of living with the emotional pain. Neither of us wants to continue to live that way. I don't know what all of this will mean for me. The thought of it feels a little uncomfortable.

"But we actually prayed together for the first time ever and told the Lord we surrendered our old ways up to Him. We each confessed that our strategies were sin and self-centeredness and we received His forgiveness all over again. Each of us told the Lord we believed we were in Him and He in us, and asked Him to bring us into intimate fellowship with Him and teach us to love each other with the mind of Christ. That was all."

Silence. My joy was full! The Lord uses times like this to encourage counselors.

I was surprised when Katrina unexpectedly reached over and took Tony's hand. Her stiff countenance had softened and she was open as she spoke, "I knew in my heart I had to verbalize to God my desire to live out of dependency on Him. Anne, you have helped me see I've mistakenly looked for 'life' from Tony and my kids. Like you said, I've entered a new land where even the language is different. It feels kind of uncertain, but it feels good, too. I've surrendered, but I am facing something I never dealt with. But I know I have to."

"Do you mean unforgiveness for the abuse from your past?" I asked.

"Yes, you know my history and how I was a victim of my father's verbal and physical abuse and his sexual advances. And you know I haven't known how to get beyond this. But I've gradually seen that just because I have been victimized at different times in my life, it doesn't make my *identity* 'a victim.' I am who I am because of who the Lord has made me as a new creation. I also have come to believe the Bible teaches that Jesus came to heal my soul and emotions and deliver me from the shame of the past by His life and truth. It is going to be up to me to receive the reality of that."

I said, "We found earlier in your sessions that your automatic guardedness and lack of trust were tied to your past abuse and fear of being hurt again. *When this is the case, it is as if you were still tied to your father and were giving him control over your life even though he passed away three years ago.* It has hindered your sexual responsiveness to Tony."

Katrina said she now understood that even though this was true, at the same time, she had also ironically looked to fill her loneliness by being *connected with* Tony! Katrina held the tissue box and wept quietly as she stared in her lap. I told them that I usually waited to address the forgiveness issue until folks have a foundation of truth. This was the perfect time to deal with it so that its influence in her life could be broken. She needed to grieve her losses and leave the past before she could cleave to Tony.

Tony, Katrina and Forgiveness

When we have unforgiveness toward another, it is giving ourselves over to be controlled by what that person has done. We could say *it is giving that individual's sinful behavior a place of emotional loyalty in our lives.*

Unforgiveness begins with the pain of rejection, unjust treatment or abuse. And it can start when someone blocks our agenda or tries to control us. When we are unforgiving, we believe we are either punishing the person who has offended us or that we are teaching him a lesson. But we bring suffering to *ourselves!* Holding unforgiveness turns out to accomplish just the opposite than we thought.

Often, we are not aware of our unforgiveness. Or if we are, we don't know that it can be the root of our anxiety, critical tongue, judgmentalism and anger toward others. Anger toward our mate can actually be the expression of unresolved hurt and bitterness toward someone from our growing-up years, perhaps a parent or another authority figure.

Katrina had tried to forgive her father in the past but she had a false understanding of what forgiveness is—as many of us do. She had believed she had forgiven if she did nice things for him, enjoyed being around him, forgot the hurt, gave him the benefit of the doubt and didn't feel angry anymore. *But none of this is certain evidence of forgiveness.*

Katrina held some of the common misconceptions of forgiveness. Other misconceptions are, "Forgiveness is excusing or justifying the past" and "forgiveness is saying what the offender did was right." As long as we carry unforgiveness, we can see our identity as victims rather than people who experienced something bad happening to us. As Katrina, we must know that *whatever happens to us does not make us who we are.*

Unforgiveness *always* results in *our* being emotionally damaged. The most important thing to know is that Jesus Christ came to heal the broken-hearted, those who have been hurt, shamed or who carry guilt.

He came to restore our damaged souls and emotions. To experience that freedom and healing, we must choose by an *act of our will* to surrender and forgive from the heart *with the attitude of Christ.*

This decision cannot be based on emotions. If we are walking after the Spirit, not demanding our presumed rights, we *will* be in a state of forgiveness toward others! Unforgiveness is sin because it is using our own strategies to try to gain satisfaction from another person. Second Corinthians 2:11 says that we must forgive so that we will not be taken advantage of by Satan.

Of course, others *should* treat us with love, fairness and respect. But the fact is, they won't. We falsely believe slights and insults somehow damage our self-esteem and strip us of our entitlements. However, since our esteem, completeness and healing are only found in Christ, we cannot hold others responsible for giving us these things we need. We must *cancel the debt* that we feel another owes us. We feel that a person who has offended us must "get his due" and that we must not let him "get away with what he did." Forgiving a person does not let him get away with anything! This is because God promises to avenge evil. We can't. He promises that vengeance belongs to Him. That paradox of Christianity is that we experience Christ's abundant life when we repay evil with good.

Tony spoke up and said, *"Before we learned all we have in counseling, I used to think if Katrina would only acknowledge what she has done to hurt me, I could forgive her. But I see now that wouldn't be forgiveness at all."* This idea is another false belief about forgiveness.

I told a short story to Tony and Katrina to illustrate the concept of forgiveness.

A short story

In Matthew 18:21–35, Jesus told His disciples a story of three men to illustrate forgiveness. The men were a king, one of his slaves and a fellow slave. The first slave had borrowed a lot of money from the king for some reason. Time went by and it was time for the king to settle his accounts. The first slave did not have the means to repay what he owed. The king told him to sell his family and all he owned to pay his debt. The slave fell at the king's feet and begged him to have patience and he would eventually repay everything he owed. The king had compassion and forgave the debt.

Soon afterward, the first slave went and seized the poor fellow slave who owed him a small amount of money and demanded he pay his debt. The fellow slave fell at the first slave's feet and begged him to have patience and he would repay. But the first slave was unwilling to have mercy and forgive in the same way the king had shown mercy toward him. And he threw his fellow slave in jail.

Someone reported this to the king. The king found the first slave and told him he was wicked because he had been forgiven of his debt and yet he did not have the mercy to forgive his fellow slave in the same manner. So, the king turned the first slave over to the tormentors. And Jesus turned to his disciples and said, "And so shall My heavenly Father also do to you, if each of you does not forgive his brother from your heart."

In this story, the King represents God, the first slave depicts you and the fellow slave is symbolic of the one whom you do not forgive. *Jesus was saying that God will allow you to experience tormentors (such as fear, depression, anxiety, rage, fatigue, physical ailments and so on when you do not forgive from your heart.*

Based on Matthew 18, the act of forgiveness binds those tormentors of the soul out of our lives. *Un*forgiveness opens the door to these tormentors, loosing them to defile us and causing us to suffer. The very power of the cross and the attitude of Christ is contained in the act of forgiveness.

In response to this parable, Tony and Katrina verbalized their forgiveness to each other. Katrina also chose to forgive her father. It was part of their overall surrender to God. Both would probably have to periodically reaffirm this choice they made until their emotions lined up.

Darryl and Mattie and Forgiveness

Darryl and Mattie had also come to the stage in counseling at which they needed to face the issue of forgiveness. Darryl said, "I can see how I have lived in unforgiveness toward both of my parents. I have lived out of fear of rejection and failure even until now, since I have felt I could never please my dad."

He elaborated, "In counseling, I became aware that both my mother and father rescued me from having to experience the consequences of my actions. I was afraid to take responsibility because of the criticism that I thought they and Mattie directed at me when I *would* try. I realize I've held unforgiveness toward Mattie for the same reasons."

In order for Darryl and Mattie to be reinforced with some of the truths regarding forgiveness, I gave the following exercise for homework. Perhaps you would like to complete it as well.

Forgiveness

According to Ephesians 4:32 and Colossians 3:12, 13, what are we called to do regarding forgiveness?

forgive others as God forgave us

How did God forgive us according to Psalm 103:12, Isaiah 43:25 and Jeremiah 31:34?

remove, blot out, forget

List what you think may be some **consequences of unforgiveness** in yourself and in your marriage:

anxiety, worry, fear

We do not want the person who has caused us pain to "get away with it!" But it causes hurt and alienation to escalate in a marriage, or in other relationships, when there is a constant effort to try to get even. We must remind ourselves that we do not have to make sure that the person who has offended us gets "his due" or is convicted of his/her wrong-doing because:

" God punishes the wicked " (Matthew 18:7; Psalm 9:16).

" justice belongs to God " (Hebrews 10:30; Romans 12:19).

When counseling couples, I often find there is a former mate and marriage relationship in which one was caught in vicious and painful cycles of relating. When this is the case, confess your part in it as sin, forgive and leave the past. It may take some time for your emotions to catch up, but it will happen. Forgiving a former spouse, just as forgiving parents and others, can release you to relate freely with your mate.

An Exercise in Forgiveness

Following is a suggestion for how you might choose to forgive. This should first be done privately. Remember that it is not necessary to verbalize this to the person who offended you, especially if they are not aware of the offense. At any rate, you need to *exercise caution about going directly* to the one toward whom you have unforgiveness. Sometimes harm can be done when the other person is not aware that you have been hurt by him.

Remember who you are in Christ and that His life, power, attitude and sufficiency are yours. Go to God with a submissive heart. Then do the following:

1. *On a sheet of paper write the name(s) of the person(s) who offended you.* Glenn

2. *Name the offense(s).* cheating

3. *Confess your unforgiveness as sin.*

4. *Decide that you will forgive. State to God and yourself that you cancel the debt.*

5. *Define what forgiveness will specifically mean for you—perhaps what attitude you will need to take in relation to the other person.* peace, trust, not fear, not be anxious

6. *Know that the offense was your opportunity to appropriate Christ's life and promises.*

You must forgive your mate for all injustice and unfairness. Let it go. Tell your mate you forgive and cancel the debt if he or she is aware of your unforgiveness.

You can also help your partner to forgive by asking if he will forgive you for any offenses he is holding against you. This may or may not mean that you are guilty of the offense. You are merely helping your mate to release you from the debt he is holding against you. This is for his good. *Apologizing* doesn't help your mate to forgive. If you have been in a habit of casually asking for forgiveness or apologizing as a way "off the hook" and then continue to do the offense again, recognize this as one of your fleshly strategies. Confess it to God, surrender yourself and leave this pattern of relating behind.

Take the responsibility of refusing to let echoes of the past rob you of the present and future. *Do not keep the hurt alive by allowing unforgiveness to frustrate God's grace in your life.* This means do not block the good things God freely gives by holding on to unforgiveness or any other strategies. Holding unforgiveness toward people from your past keeps the hurt alive in your emotions, and it will affect every area of your life, especially your marriage.

At this point, I asked Darryl and Mattie to turn to each other and confess any unforgiveness toward the other and then to ask the other, "Will you forgive me for...?"

I left the room so they could have this as private time with each other and God. When I quietly returned, they were holding each other, tears streaming down their faces. After some time passed, Mattie spoke, "I feel so light, as if something heavy has been lifted from me." She didn't seem like the steel magnolia anymore.

Darryl said, "I feel clean and free. This is definitely a significant time. But I know emotions change. What happens if next week we don't *feel* like we have forgiven?" When a couple goes through this choice to forgive in my office, I tell them it is a definite time they can look back on and remind themselves of what happened, regardless of what their emotions later tell them.

If they feel the hurt again about the same offenses, they must reaffirm their decision of forgiveness regardless of how many times it takes. If someone does hurt them again, Scripture says that we are to forgive seventy times seven. This is symbolic; it means we are to forgive a limitless number of times. You and I will fall down many times in our relationship and so will our mates. So, we must forgive and give them space to make mistakes just as we want them to do the same for us.

> ## *What if I don't "feel" like I have forgiven?*
>
> When you are feeling hurt and angry and make the decision to forgive, there are times when the pain and bitter emotional feelings will leave instantly but, often, the feelings subside as you continue to walk in obedience reaffirming your choice to forgive. You have already learned that you do not make decisions *based* on your emotions, but on the truth. Feelings may or may not be reliable indicators of whether you have forgiven. However, if you are having hurt or bitter feelings on an ongoing basis and continually dwell on the offense, there is a good chance that you haven't begun to forgive.

Latoya and Forgiveness

Latoya had experienced much disappointment and hurt in her relationship with Joe and the emotions had intensified when Joe refused to continue with counseling. She had said in the beginning, "Well, I have a right to be bitter over Joe's not being involved in the marriage!" I had tried to help Latoya see that while she felt bitterness was a right she was holding on to, it was something that was *destroying her*! Latoya had struggled with this issue because her family and friends said she should never forgive Joe.

Among various reasons that people don't forgive are: pride, fear of being hurt again, the other person isn't sorry for what he did, feeling one would be a hypocrite if he didn't *feel* forgiving, and fear of emotions that might surface as a result of forgiving.

Through the counseling process, Latoya realized that she had not forgiven her mother. When Latoya was young, her mother was vindictive and would manipulate by emotionally cutting off the kids and Latoya's dad when they did not do things her way. Being strong and independent, Latoya had stuffed her anger and resentment about this.

We do not know what we do to *ourselves* by holding onto bitterness. Scripture says a root of bitterness defiles many. It definitely cripples us. Scientific studies have shown that bitterness and unforgiveness weaken our immune system and can lead to the occurrence of many serious physical problems such as cancer, arthritis, physical pain and infections. It definitely leads to anger, depression, revenge, gossip, self-righteousness, insensitivity, guardedness and not being able to receive love.

Latoya had made the choice earlier to surrender her controls to God. But she knew she would never be free of her anger and depression unless she decided to forgive Joe and her mother and learn to love with the mind of Christ. She had to realize that when we forgive others, they may never change but their actions will have no more power over us. This was something Latoya resolved on her own in her time alone with God. She was beginning to renew her mind but walking it out would take time, often with two steps forward and one step backward.

The couples and Latoya were making decisions *to break destructive ties by humility and forgiveness.* This was a most important step in beginning to respond to others with Christ's attitude. Now was the time to coach them in the necessity of also leaving other emotional loyalties behind. They needed to walk away from *old inappropriate ties* to mother, fathers, siblings—even children and friends! When we do this, we are yielding fleshly strategies, and we are forgiving. **In doing so, we draw boundaries for ourselves** so we are no longer controlled by others.

Leaving and Cleaving: Divided loyalties

In many cases of significant marital discord, there is a divided loyalty, where a mate is more loyal to other family members, a job, or outside interests than to the husband or wife. When the loyalty is to parents, they have direct access into the marriage relationship! Or controlling grandparents can become improperly aligned with one or more of the grandchildren, which causes interference in the marriage. This dependency and enmeshment is often is a result of a myth, which is, "That is what family is all about."

In situations such as these, I tell my couples it is as though the object of the loyalty attachment sits between the husband and wife on my counseling sofa, dividing them!

When situations like these are the case, the family is not properly *structured* or *framed* together, there are no proper *boundaries* between certain individuals and they are emotionally dependent on each other. Other family members feel left out.

The Lord has ordained a way that the universe, the family and the body of Christ is to be properly framed together (Ephesians 2:21) so that everything will work right and according to His purpose. The key to a family's structure being right begins with the marital partner being in a right relationship with his or her own immediate family and with each other. *This is a spiritual issue* with the Lord. Jesus knew well that these improper attachments would happen and He specifically addressed the issue. His words are recorded in Mark 10:6–9 and Matthew 19:4–6 when He said that *we are to leave parents so that we might cleave to a spouse.*

This *leaving* is related to a person losing his fleshly life and the old strategies formed early in the context of the family. This word *leave* can mean "forsake." We must forsake all other loyalty ties to follow Christ. This is the death to self that must happen in all of life's relationships, including marriage.

This does not mean that we leave or forsake the relationships *themselves,* because each member of the body of Christ needs every other member for encouragement and edification as the body functions properly. We are to attend to our relationships in a mature way, in love—not dependency. Often, an adult child will move thousands of miles away in an unconscious effort to cut off ties or any influence from family controls but, alas, he finds that he has taken his attachment to them and their values with him in his own variety of "flesh." *Leaving* involves no longer having to prove your worthiness to your parents and having to have acceptance from them in the way you live and manage your families.

Remember: When you begin to think and respond differently, perhaps no longer being dependent on friends and family, they will likely react and may unconsciously try to sabotage what you are doing and force you back into your old ways. This is because your change can be threatening to *their* emotional security! It can be helpful to explain to those family and friends something of the spiritual reasons for your decisions to make your spouse your number one loyalty.

Chapter 19

At Home: The Point Man and the Virtuous Woman

> On the Map: In Canaan. We will look at the "roles" of husband and wife in this context. Our couples have begun a new way of relating in a new land.

Marital *Roles*?

Home at last! The travelers' journeys had finally led them to the land of their inheritance. All had crossed the river and were in Canaan. They had found a new highway there that had been entered by a toll of humility and self-sacrifice. Staying on this toll-road assured safety, peace and joy and would require making ongoing choices.

To remain on this road and live in this unfamiliar territory, each needed to have clarified what is referred to as "the roles" of husband and wife so they could continue in faith if they were ever questioned or attacked. I will use the case of George and Carol to illustrate a common misunderstanding about "roles."

George and Carol

Last year when George and Carol first came to counseling, I asked each how they would define their problem. George said, "If she would just submit to me, give me respect, and not try to be independent in her thinking, things would be fine."

Carol had replied, "If he would only at least listen to my opinions, we wouldn't have the conflicts we have. He tries to give solutions and that's not what I need. I try to be responsible and make him feel good, but nothing works and my efforts aren't appreciated. Something must be wrong with *me* since he is so irritable. I cry a lot and am confused as to why our relationship isn't working."

George had revealed, "Members of my family have always been strong Christian examples. As head of the family, my father always ran things and kept my mother under submission. My mother lived her role. She kept house and stayed in her place. Carol needs to understand that my job is to hold things together, straighten her out if she is wrong and give the solutions. I am accountable to God for her."

A predominant myth that George held was that his worth as a man was related to his role as head. He believed that headship and authority meant being in control and seeing to it that the job got done, by force, if necessary.

Carol's strategies, which she had learned early in life, included the belief that, as a submissive wife, she was responsible for George's emotional well-being or lack of it. Well, George had the same belief! Carol was compliant and easy to be around and actually believed she was responsible for everyone with whom she had a relationship.

Carol was hurting and frustrated because she had valid opinions and ways of doing things that were never expressed without being shot down. One of Carol's myths was that her fulfillment was dependent on being validated for her opinions and being appreciated for the people-pleasing things she did. Many of their marital difficulties were rooted in the wrong beliefs that she and George held about the "roles" of husband and wife.

George and Carol had a hard time in the beginning of counseling as they expressed these beliefs with much hurt, confusion and resentment. As counseling progressed, however, they received the truths they heard. The couple had discovered their myths, the purpose of adversity and responding with the mind of Christ and how to set their minds and not live out of emotions. Each had just made the choice to surrender, and the question of "roles" needed to be addressed.

After I opened our session with prayer, the first thing George said was, "I've been sharing what we are learning in counseling with a friend who is a Christian. This week, he brought up a subject that has been an issue between Carol and me. My friend reacted when I told him that the correct response to one's spouse should be one of servanthood and sacrificing one's controls. He asked how that fit with the fact that, being head of the household, the husband's role is to be the one in control and see to it that the wife submits. This subject needs to be clarified for us."

Carol turned to me with, "I've heard that the husband is to be the "umbrella of protection," and if the wife gets out from under it, she will not be safe. If we are to make a home in this 'new and unfamiliar territory,' as you call it, we need to make sure we understand this thing about roles!"

I said there has been a tendency to think that "roles" are defined by specific *behaviors* such as who handles the money, who administers discipline, who does the yard work, who does the housework or who initiates prayer and Bible study and so on. We bring assumptions into marriage and, when our expectations aren't realized, conflicts arise. Many of our false suppositions are rooted in religious views of certain Scriptures that may have been taken out of context, or the views may have come from a transliteration of certain verses.

I showed George and Carol the following list that reflects some beliefs concerning the "roles" of husbands and wives. I asked them to identify those that they had held to. Which of them do *you* believe are scriptural?

Which of the following beliefs do you think are valid?

The husband must be:

1. The strong one
2. The decisive one
3. The leader
4. The priest
5. The authority
6. The initiator

The wife must be:

1. The dependent one
2. Free from decisions
3. The completer
4. The nurturing one
5. The one to submit
6. The responder

7. The one responsible	7. The silent one
8. The dominant one	8. The helper
9. The protector	9. The influencer

Understanding "roles": In context

Often the "roles" of husband and wife are based on the terms *headship* and *submission*. I helped George and Carol look at the context in which the terms *head* and *submit* are used in Ephesians regarding the husband and wife in order to dispel any wrong ideas about marital "roles."

In the first three chapters, Paul reminds all believers of *what they have* and of *who they are in Christ— so they would not be ignorant of their abundant riches in Him.* Here, Paul stated his desire that believers experience the good things from their inheritance in Christ.

In order for them to *enjoy* these riches, Paul said four things must happen:

1) Christ must dwell in their hearts by faith;

2) they must be rooted and grounded in love;

3) they must know the love of Christ that surpasses knowledge; and

4) they must be filled with all the fullness of God. So he prayed that these things would happen (Ephesians 3:16-19).

In the last three chapters, Paul exhorts believers to walk worthy of their calling. He reminds them that they were created unto good works and they should walk in them. He knew that only by this walk after the Spirit would they enjoy the fullness that was *already theirs* in the Lord. In chapter four, he begins to tell these believers how this walk is to happen—what it is to look like.

In the fifth chapter, he continues to encourage them to live in this way. He tells them to be imitators of Christ and to walk circumspectly as who they are in Christ. In effect, he says that they are to walk like God or be imitators of God. I have talked at length with these couples about putting on the attitude of Christ as in Philippians 2:5–8. This is what Paul was referring to when he said to walk like God. He tells them that they *are* light in the Lord, now they are to *walk as* children of light, to walk as who they are!

In Ephesians 5:1–6, 9, Paul then proceeds to describe characteristics of this walk. He describes it as: 1) a walk in love; 2) a walk in light; 3) a walk in wisdom understanding what the will of the Lord is; and 4) being filled with the Spirit. Then he indicates that evidences of being filled with the Spirit are a) singing and making melody in their heart; b) giving thanks always for all things; and c) submitting to one another in the fear (reverence) of God.

Paul continues by saying that this being filled as they mutually submit to one another is to happen in three types of relationships. These relationships are between 1) husbands and wives; 2) parents and children; and 3) bondservants and masters.

Something struck a chord in Carol as she listened to this. She said, "You've taught us that if we surrender to God and put on that attitude of a servant and humility, accepting our mate as he is, Christ will meet our needs and fulfill us. You said if we choose to go this way, we'd enjoy the blessings God has given us. *Paul is saying the same thing here!* I think I'm seeing the very truths you've taught being stated a little differently by Paul."

I was excited that Carol had made the connection. I related that this being filled is not something *we* can do but is something *we allow* to be done to us. *Be filled* is a command to believers. It is from the Greek word, *pleroma*, which is a passive imperative (command). *God will fill us as we empty ourselves and it will be lived out by our submitting to one another.* This mutual submission refers to *all relationships* in the body of Christ but Paul *begins* by describing its application in the husband/wife relationship.

To further clarify the meaning of the words *head* and *submit* for George and Carol, I shared the following Scripture and comments.

Headship:

- ▲ "For the husband is *head* of the wife, as also Christ is head of the church; and He is the Savior of the body" (Ephesians 5:23 NKJV; my emphasis).

- ▲ "Husbands, love your wives, just as Christ loved the church and *gave Himself up* for her" (Ephesians 5:25, my emphasis).

225

The Greek word for *head* in some passages could be thought of as meaning "the source," but in Ephesians 5:23, it carries the definition that is closer to the ancient military term *point man*. Originally, the point man was a soldier who volunteered to be a servant and lead out in front of the others in battle to scout for the enemy but, in doing so, he took death or *gave himself up* on their behalf. There is still a point man in the military today. While the concept of *authority* is connected to the term *point man*, in the kingdom of God the meaning of authority is exemplified in the sacrificial life and death of Christ.

A description of Christ's role was that He took death for us. He was the Point Man. The role of Christ as *head* was to *give Himself up* for the church. In order to do this, He had to relinquish His rights, protections, privileges and so on. He *led* in this. The husband who is *head* of the wife should also engage in this kind of *leadership*! This is the standard that the Lord commands for a personal walk after the Spirit. Notice that Scripture does not say the husband is the *head* of the *household*, but of the *wife*.

Jeff Van Vonderan, in his book, *Families Where Grace Is In Place* said,

In this world *leader* means *boss*, the one in charge, the one in front. But Jesus says leaders are servants (Matthew 23:11 and Luke 22:26). It is the same way with the word *head*. Paul is saying, "Everywhere else 'head' means 'boss', chief executive officer, commander. But in the kingdom of God, the head is the person who comes under others, serving building and being ready to die for them" (p. 85).

Scripture says whoever would be *first, chief,* or the *greater*, will be last and the servant (Matthew 20:26-27; 23:11, Mark 9:35; 10:43-44).

In 1 Corinthians 11:13 and Ephesians 5:25-27, the *head* is the one responsible for leading in sacrifice and death to the flesh on behalf of his wife. This is true servanthood and being conformed to the image of Christ. It is servant leadership.

In their book, *Intimate Allies,* Allender and Longman see the husband or *head* as the "vassal king" who was responsible to the "great king" over him and who was the *first to sacrifice himself* on behalf of the inhabitants of the kingdom.

226

Head = Point Man

The Greek word for *head* in some passages could be thought of as meaning "the source," but in Ephesians 5:23, it carries the definition that is closer to the ancient military term, *point man*. Originally, the point man was a soldier who volunteered to be a servant and lead out in front of the others in battle to scout for the enemy but, in doing so, he took death or *gave himself up* on their behalf. There is still a point man in the military today. While the concept of *authority* is connected to the term *point man*, in the kingdom of God the meaning of authority is exemplified in the sacrificial life and death of Christ.

A description of Christ's role was that He took death for us. He was the Point Man. The role of Christ as *head* was to *give Himself up* for the church. In order to do this, He sacrificed His rights, protections, privileges. He *led* in this. The husband being *head* of the wife is to also engage in this kind of *leadership*.

Submission:

▲ "Wives, be subject (*submit*) to your own husbands as to the Lord" (Ephesians 5:22).

▲ "But *as the church is subject* to Christ, so also the wives ought to be to their husbands in everything" (Ephesians 5:24; my emphasis).

This word *subject* means "submit" and has the meaning of *voluntary* deference to another. It is not something that is gained by force or domination. Submission would include a letting go of one's rights, fleshly protections and patterns in preference of, or in relation to, another. This *is* the same submission or surrender to the Lord that *anyone* does to walk after the Spirit. True submission is not "people-pleasing" compliance. That is false submission!

The phrase "as unto the Lord" is key in defining the wife's submission. This submission is the sacrifice of old strategies while putting on the mind of Christ, which is His will for *all* of us. This submission is the losing of our fleshly life, or the death to the flesh, that is required for anyone following Christ, as well as for living in the marital relationship. *There is not one submission for marriage and another unto Christ.* It is all the same. Godly submission is godly submission. Therefore, it could be said that the degree to which one is submitted to God is the degree to which one is submitted in the marriage relationship.

Some would say that the words *submission* and *headship* carry much of the same meaning regarding voluntary deference and servanthood. However, although the term *head* would include a godly attitude of submission and also a sacrifice of rights and privileges and so on, it is more inclusive than the word *submit*. As the head and the one who leads out in death to self, the husband would also have the responsibility of providing for the family and making final decisions where agreement could not otherwise be reached and of providing for the family (1 Timothy 5: 8).

The exercising of *both headship* and *submission* could be described as the putting on of that attitude of Christ in Philippians 2:5–8. Within this Scripture is a picture of humility, death to self and the truth that *all* should be in humble submission to each other. This is the *same* principle of mutual submission taught in Ephesians 5:21 through Ephesians 6:9. Jesus said that if anyone desires to be first (important or "boss"), he must be last of all and servant of all. This is indeed a mystery, that paradox of Christianity. Note that one's submission does not make the one submitted to, the authority!

Douglas Anderson, commenting on mutual submission in the *Holman Bible Dictionary* says,

> The admonition to mutual submission in Ephesians 5:21 applies to all relationships within the church (Eph. 5:25—6:10) and in Christian marriage (Eph. 5:21–33). Both Paul and Peter's use of submission refers to voluntary submission in a loving relationship, not the forced subjection to authority in a military organization. The Biblical references say submit yourself to one another, not subject the other person to yourself (Eph. 5:21, 22, 24; Col. 3:18; 1 Peter 3: 1). In such a relationship, the husband's role as head is modeled after the self-giving of Christ (Eph. 5:23, 25, 28–30; Phil. 2:1–11; Col. 3:19; 1 Peter 3:7).

Mutual submission carries the meaning of mutual sacrifice. This type of submission is the whole idea found in Luke 17:33, "Whoever seeks to keep his life will lose it, and whoever loses his life will preserve it." Submission is not only voluntary deference to another but it is giving up the pursuit of anything other than Christ to bring contentment. Yes, we long for our marital relationship to bring us satisfaction, but we must not demand that our spouse give what only the Lord can give. However , He *may* choose to give it *through* our mate.

The term *be subject* in the Greek is *hupostasis,* which means "to arrange yourself underneath." *We live out our obedience to Christ by being subject to one another, preferring the other above ourselves and arranging ourselves underneath them in humility, self-sacrifice and servant-hood.* This is being conformed to His image and is the Lord's will for each in marriage and in all of life's relationships. This is that paradox of dying to live and losing to find. It is when our will is lost in His will.

Frequently, a people-pleaser who has been *falsely submissive or externally compliant* (and angry because of feeling that he/she has been taken advantage of and not appreciated), becomes resistant to pleasing the spouse in an effort to surrender those old strategies. This is also done in an effort to not feel controlled anymore. This person is confused about true submission and it seems that a heart attitude of submission would make him/her a "doormat."

When this happens, I explain that when one knows who he is in Christ and that the Lord is his emotional protection, and *then voluntarily* arranges himself under the other, he is not a doormat or being controlled! Whether one is a doormat is dependent on one's mind-set. To an observer, the pleasing behavior may *look* the same as it did when it was done after the flesh, but it is not the same thing because the heart attitude has changed. True submission would be what Scripture refers to as "living works," while false submission would be "dead works."

The way Christ is to be lived out in marriage is identical to the way all believers are told to follow Him! Christ said if anyone would follow Him they must leave mother and father, take up their cross and deny themselves. In Ephesians 5:31,32, Christ and the church are depicted in marriage by two leaving parents and cleaving with each other obviously in the context of submission. It is the same thing. It is just the Christian life being lived out in marriage, which is a picture of Christ and the church and an illustration of the cross.

Wellington Boone, in his book, *Your Wife is Not Your Momma*, says that the scriptural standard is not who is *being* served but who is *doing* the serving.

George said, "I have never in my life heard the terms *head* and *submit* explained this way. I can see it clearly and can explain it to my friend. But I have a request. Please help me understand the religious cliché, "A spouse is to put God first, the spouse second, and everything else third."

I asked him, *"How do you think this is possible in the context of everything we have learned?"* He was puzzled and struggled to answer my question. I said, "Consider this. When a mate is surrendered to God, responding with an attitude of humility and self-sacrifice as he relates with his spouse, **he IS putting God first and his spouse first as well!**"

George had a request. It was for me
to explain the religious cliché,

*"A spouse is to put God first, the other spouse second,
and everything else third."*

I asked him, *"How do you think this is possible in the
context of everything we have learned?"* He was puzzled
and struggled to answer my question. I replied,
"Consider this. When a mate is surrendered to God,
responding with an attitude of humility and self-
sacrifice as he relates with his spouse, *he IS putting
God first and his spouse first as well!"*

This IS living out one's obedience to God in marriage.

Something to think about:

Some have taught that it is the wife who has the tremendous responsibility to "set the tone" in the marriage, that her husband's well-being and/or behavior is a reflection of, or dependent on, her attitude.

Others believe that if the wife must "set the tone" for the relationship, that it would put her in the role of being the leader or, at least, in a position of control. Or that it would be her taking the responsibility (and not her husband) for *his* spiritual and emotional well-being. First Peter 3:1–2 is the Scripture reference that many use when they say it is the wife's "duty to influence" her husband in this way. This Scripture says that if there is a husband who is not obedient to the Word, the wife's submissive and chaste conduct may win him over. As we have indicated, submissiveness is the *typical attitude required by God in any situation*—without any motive except obedience to God. And this *may* or *may not* influence the husband. Influence is *not* manipulation. A book can "influence" a person by its very *being*!

Ephesians 5:26 is another Scripture that is often understood by husbands to mean that they have the responsibility to teach their wives and make sure they are spiritually clean and behaving godly. It is a completion of the thought in verse 25, which tells the husbands to love and give themselves up for their wives as Christ did for the church (v. 26) so that He might sanctify and cleanse her by the washing of water by the Word. Often, husbands have tried to force their wives to comply with behaviors that they believe are submissive. But true sacrificial giving up of himself for his wife is *in itself* the sanctifying influence.

This is like the wife's chaste behavior *in itself* being the thing that *might* win over the husband. There are no guarantees and her chaste behavior cannot be with that motive! Husbands and wives are both called to holiness, which is all that is required for being an influence on the other!

After pointing out the above truths to George and Carol, I explained that spiritual leadership or *headship* does not *mean* teaching, keeping another in line, guiding and so on. There is nothing wrong and everything right with Spirit-led teaching and initiating study of the Word. However, spiritual leadership or living as *head* does not require this. Any activity or behavior such as this must be done in the context of death to the flesh and putting on the attitude of Christ.

In reply to George's comment that he believed as head he was to be accountable to God for his wife, I pointed to the Scripture that says *each is to give account to God for himself* (Romans 14:12). I further emphasized that nothing he could *do* would make him head! A husband *is* head of the wife because God *made* him head. He may not always fulfill the walk as head, but he is still head.

In the beginning, both George and Carol had been under the impression that submission meant *dependency*. Submission, as we have seen, *does not* mean dependency, nor does it mean co-dependent behaviors. Carol learned that her own emotions had been dependent upon others' responses when she became aware of frequently saying, "I was so hurt when they did such and such." As a result, she began to take responsibility in Christ for her own well-being in marriage as well as other relationships.

George was struggling with the belief that he was *entitled* to Carol submitting to him as God commands. It was revealing to him that there are no promises to him that she *will* obey God and that *he is not entitled* to her obeying God and to walking as she should. And he must not *demand* this of her. Of course, this is also true for Carol regarding her emotional demands that George behave toward her as the Lord commands.

I recall when George finally understood about surrender and responding with the attitude of a servant. He surprised me when he said, "I saw in the counseling session last week that I must not only sacrifice my *sinful* ways *but also my ways that aren't sinful in choosing to give myself up for Carol.*" For George to see this was a huge thing and now he understood even better how it related to marriage.

Carol had more questions, "Is the husband supposed to be the wife's umbrella of protection, as I have heard some say?" My reply was that God is to be the protection for each individual, and I wasn't aware of any Scriptures that indicate the husband is commanded to be his wife's protection as part of his "role."

Regarding the question of the husband being the authority over the wife, I stated I did not know of any scriptural evidence regarding this. This belief is taken from the Scriptures exhorting the wife to submit.

Submission does not *make* the one submitted to, the authority, for each member of the body of Christ is to submit to the other.

I pointed out to Carol that the only verses related to husbands and wives having authority over each other are the ones stating that each has power over the other's body to sexually satisfy the other. These Scriptures indicate they are not to deprive one another sexually and each should live out their submission and obedience to God in pleasing the other in this way within marriage (1 Corinthians 7:2–6). The apostle Paul says this because it falls under one's choosing to love and please the other rather than be immoral.

After having their questions about marital "roles" answered, they wanted more coaching in how to show love toward their mate. This would come next in the counseling process.

Chapter 20

Love Has Everything to Do with It

On the Map: In Canaan. Learning to live in a new land and enjoy the abundance there.

The night wore black velvet. After a long day at work, we were quietly reflective as we traveled home among the racing lights on I-985. Vinson turned on the radio and we caught a song with the phrase, "What does love have to do with it?" chasing itself to a repetitive beat. Glancing at me he said, "Love has everything to do with it, doesn't it?

A calm gratefulness filled me because I knew that *he* knew what love is. He has practiced love longer than I have, I think. Not always, but longer than I have. And he has had the perfect opportunity for it. My husband knows that love is found in the attitudes and responses that have been taught in this book. He understands that love is humility, honoring and self-sacrifice, especially in the face of a trial. He loves because he knows God will protect him and meet his needs. He knows that "the LORD has His way In the whirlwind and in the storm" and "He does according to His will in the host of heaven And among the inhabitants of the earth" (Nahum 1:3 NKJV; Daniel 4:35). Not that he doesn't ever forget it, but he *knows* it. And he trusts God.

Tony and Katrina

Tony and Katrina's hearts were softened and yielded to God as they returned to one of their counseling sessions. Tony spoke, "I believe we are at a point where we need you to help us mentally walk through some typical situations in which we have had conflicts. Coach us in learning some practical ways that we can show love."

"Tony," I responded, "First, I want to give you two some hard copies of Scriptures to take with you so you can meditate on them and consider for yourselves how to respond to each other in love." Following are the Scriptures I shared with them. These can be helpful reminders when learning to live out love with each other.

Some Scriptures to remember regarding husbands and wives:

1. 1 Corinthians 7:32–34 — *Both are to consider ways to please each other.*

2. Genesis 2:18 — *The **wife** is created as a suitable helper.*

3. Ephesians 5:24 — *The **wife** is to be subject to her husband.*

4. Ephesians 5:25 — *The **husband** is to give himself up for his wife.*

5. 1 Peter 3:7 — *The **husband** is to live with his wife with understanding.*

6. 1 Peter 3:7 — *The **husband** is to give his wife honor.*

7. 1 Timothy 5:8 — *The **husband** is to provide for his family.*

8. Ephesians 5:33 — *The **wife** is to be respectful toward her husband.*

9. Ephesians 5:21 — *Both are to submit to the other. (Also 1 Peter 5:5.)*

Below is a chart showing a "Matrix of Marital Roles and Responsibilities" © 1996, 2002 Vernon Terrell. Used by Permission.

This chart is an outstanding way to reference the scriptural admonitions to husbands and wives shown above. You may want to look up all of the references.

Husband to Wife	Reference (Husband)	Reference (Wife)	Wife to Husband
Submit	Eph. 5:21; Phil. 2:5-8*	Eph. 5:21-24; Col. 3:18; Titus 2:5	Submit
Love	Eph. 5:25, 33: Col. 3:19; Phil. 2:5-8 *	Titus 2:4-5	Love
Live with under-standing	1 Peter 3:7	Eph. 5:33	Respect
Become one flesh	Gen. 2:24; Eph. 5:31	Gen. 2:24; Eph. 5:31	Become one flesh
Please	1 Cor. 7:33	1 Cor. 7:34	Please
Fulfill duty	1 Cor. 7:3-4	1 Cor. 7:3-4	Fulfill duty

* Scriptures apply to both spouses, however the husband is head of the wife as Christ is head of the church, therefore cited under the husband (husband is commanded to love the wife as Christ loved the church).

When love appears, it looks like this:

When Christ's love appears through us, it: (1 Corinthians 13:4–7).

- ❏ Is patient
- ❏ Is not jealous
- ❏ Is not arrogant
- ❏ Does not seek its own way
- ❏ Does not record wrongs suffered
- ❏ Rejoices in the truth
- ❏ Believes all things
- ❏ Is kind
- ❏ Does not brag
- ❏ Does not act unbecomingly
- ❏ Is not easily provoked
- ❏ Does not enjoy unrighteousness
- ❏ Bears (not "tolerates") all things
- ❏ Endures all things

When love appears, this fruit of the Spirit is evident in and through us:
(Galatians 5:22)

❏ Love
❏ Joy
❏ Peace
❏ Patience
❏ Kindness
❏ Goodness
❏ Faithfulness
❏ Gentleness
❏ Self-control

A wife is to be:

❏ Trustworthy   (Proverbs 31:11)
❏ Respecting her husband   (Ephesians 5: 33)
❏ Submissive   (Ephesians 5: 22)
❏ Chaste   (Titus 2: 5)
❏ Gentle   (1 Peter 3: 4)
❏ A helper   (Genesis 2: 18)

A husband is to:

❏ Understand his wife, giving her honor   (1 Peter 3:7)
❏ Provide for her   (1 Timothy 5: 8)
❏ Praise his wife   (Proverb 31: 28)
❏ Give himself up for her   (Ephesians 5:25)
❏ Not be bitter toward her   (Colossians 3: 19)

Each, in his behaviors toward the other, is to: (1 Peter 2:18, 3: 2; Galatians 5:22; Ephesians 5:9; Philippians 2:3,4)

❏ Not speak deception or lie
❏ Be tenderhearted
❏ When reviled, not revile in return
❏ Be honorable
❏ Not return evil for evil
❏ Not provoke the other
❏ Be compassionate
❏ Not envy the other
❏ Be courteous
❏ Not threaten
❏ Esteem the other better than himself

Each is to think continually on whatever is: (Philippians 4:8).

❏ True	❏ Noble	❏ Just
❏ Pure	❏ Lovely	❏ Of good report
❏ Virtuous	❏ Praiseworthy	

Each is to be:

❏ Humble	❏ Meek	❏ Kind
❏ Patient	❏ Gentle	❏ Peaceable
❏ Joyful	❏ Faithful	❏ Good
❏ A servant	❏ Emptied of himself	

(Hebrews 12:11; Philippians 4:5; 1 Peter 3:1, 5; Colossians 3; 12; James 4:6, 10, 17; Philippians 2:5–8)

Remember that God is love, and we cannot love another by struggling to make it happen. It happens only by our surrender, our choosing to have Christ's attitude and allowing His life to love through us

Katrina commented on these handouts saying, "I really desire to see us walk toward making this kind of love a reality in our marriage. At the same time, I know my concern must be on *my* walk and not on Tony's responses." Then she quizzed, "The part about my seeing to it that I respect Tony. How is it possible if he doesn't do things that *deserve* respect?" I was glad Katrina asked the question about respect because people seem to have a poor understanding of this concept.

I answered Katrina, "Each member of the Body of Christ is to be respectful of the other. Your respecting Tony, or anyone else, is *your walking and responding in a respectful manner.* This is all part of your having that heart attitude of humility, servanthood, kindness, gentleness and so on toward Tony that we have discussed. It really has nothing to do with whether he *deserves* this or not."

Her reaction was one of contemplation, then surprise. "I have never thought of it like that. What a revelation to me! This puts *all* you have taught us into more of a correct perspective."

Tony interjected, "I have never seen it that way, either. Your explanation helps me understand more clearly how all of these truths fit together."

The good report

Katrina became very still in the session. She didn't finger her earring. Her long legs were crossed, but her foot never jiggled once. When I asked her what her thoughts were, she said she had suddenly become aware that her talking with her family about Tony's ways was not love. She revealed, "I guess I wasn't being respectful. I realize what I was saying was *factual*, but it was not based on God's *truth*. It wasn't lovely or worthy of praise and not the good report that we are told to think on in Philippians 4:8. It was my keeping account of the wrongs done to me. I was focusing on the wrongs! 1 Corinthians 13 says that love doesn't record wrongs. Maybe I was being disloyal to Tony by sharing our personal problems with my mother and sisters."

I was *thrilled* that Katrina was convicted of this. Proverb 17:9 tells us that love covers transgressions rather than exposing them. *In fact, it was gossip*, and the same Scripture says that gossip, or repeating a matter, separates closest friends. Gossip is not love, *even if what is said is true*. We are also told that the words of a talebearer are like tasty trifles, and where there is no talebearer, the strife ceases! A talebearer reveals secrets, but the person of a faithful spirit conceals a matter. Furthermore, a person who opens his lips in this way shall have destruction (Proverbs 11:13; 13:3b; 16:28; 18:8; 26:20, 22). The world may say this is being "in denial," but Scripture says this is love and godliness.

We are not to lie but speak the truth in love. This does not mean to say everything that comes into your head; but speak those things that are gentle and worthy of praise. Lying is a self-protection; people do it to build self-worth. If one has been in a habit of lying, it may seem strange at first to allow the Holy Spirit to remind you to let go of the old ways.

Seek to please

As we continued to go over the handouts containing the Scriptures on love and godly attitudes of husbands and wives, Tony commented, "All of these Scripture references just confirm what you have been telling us about allowing the attitude of Christ to be worked in us. It certainly will be choosing to live a life of giving."

"Yes, and if you do show that kind of love to Katrina, you will be allowing God to meet her needs *through* you. The Lord desires that mates be so yielded and self-sacrificial in their relationship with each other that He would use each to meet many of the other's needs. But a point I have often made is that one spouse isn't entitled to the other being God's conduit. Each must rely on the Lord to meet needs however He chooses," I said.

Tony replied, "One of the Scriptures you shared with us says that we are to seek to please our spouse. I don't think I really know how."

I replied to Tony, "I will occasionally have a mate in counseling tell me that he or she *is* trying to please the spouse and then tell me the ways of attempting to do this. It is surprising to discover that those certain things weren't what his or her partner even cared about or wanted! We often give our spouse what says love to US and not to them. We can remedy this by asking our mate what would say love to him."

Please note that there is a big difference in seeking to please and being a "people-pleaser." The former reflects a walk after the Spirit and the latter a walk after the flesh.

Tony grew as he realized that even though each is to seek to please the other with behaviors that say love to them, *the outcome is not to be the focus.* In other words, there are no promises that Katrina would be pleased *or that Tony would receive anything in return.* I want to help couples learn to be aware of what is important to their mate. And there are ways of doing this.

When couples understand the truths already presented in this book, then Gary Chapman's book, *The Five Love Languages*, can be tremendously helpful in learning what says love to the other person—his *love language.* It is not intended to be read with the selfish focus of being entitled to *get* something from the other. I recommend reading it to discover your partner's language of love.

Giving love gifts: The languages of love

Giving a love gift is self-sacrificial and it may be something that is not convenient for you to do. *After all, loving self-sacrifice is usually inconvenient.* When you give a love gift, it may be unfamiliar territory for you. *When giving gifts of love, you will exhibit the characteristics of love that have just been mentioned.* **When you give love gifts, you forfeit the "right" to be resentful or complain.**

You need to understand that love gifts may *or* may not be received by your spouse in the way you would like. But God honors those who give love gifts. A love gift is not what says love to you, but it is something that says love to your spouse. You are to do nothing out of selfish motives but consider the other better than yourself. And certain people have to train themselves in *receiving* love gifts.

According to Dr. Gary Chapman, each of us has developed a *love language.* Our love language is our tendency to express love and caring toward others in certain ways and our expectation that others express caring toward us in similar ways. According to Dr. Gary Chapman the Five Love Languages are: (1) *Words of affirmation;* (2) *Quality time;* (3) *Receiving gifts;* (4) *Acts of service;* and (5) *Physical touch.* I highly recommend that you learn your partner's "love language" so you can give to them in a meaningful way. When your partner wants to learn your "love language," remember the purpose is not for you to demand that your spouse give you what you want!

Build communication skills: A love gift

I explained to Tony that one way to understand what says love to Katrina would be to ask her what she needs and wants. And to *listen to her.* First Peter 3:7 says that husbands are to dwell with their wives with understanding and in doing so, one gives his wife honor. When he does this, his prayers won't be hindered.

Everyone desires to be heard and attended to but, all too often, we do not communicate what we mean. When we walk after old fleshly strategies, *our wishes are expressed as hints, complaints, or accusations, and our needs are stated as demands.* Old strategies say, "You never...," "You should...," etc. We speculate, "mind read," and assume what our mates mean or why they behave the way they do. Things escalate into a tug-of-war, the old familiar power struggles of one-upmanship over who is right, who did what when and who gives the most. We invalidate the other. All of this leads into pursuing and withdrawing behaviors.

Along with a commitment to walk with a surrendered attitude, relying on the Lord to satisfy our neediness, we need to learn better communication skills. Yes, this is sacrificial love.

All behavior—not just verbal—is communication. Knowledge and understanding of another comes by listening and observing. Even though we communicate in many ways, we develop good *understanding* by a *verbal* system. This may mean asking questions about your mate's concerns and desires. This does not mean nagging a person if he/she doesn't want to talk! It probably will mean reflective listening to clarify and better understand what message is being sent so you can *avoid assuming* wrong intentions.

This is extremely important, because we come from different backgrounds where one person may have learned that a certain statement or behavior had a certain meaning while the spouse comes from a different upbringing where the same action may have meant something entirely different!

Judson J. Swihart, in his little booklet, *Communication in Marriage*, relates that early in his marriage he and his wife went shopping.

> She looked at many household accessories and said, "You know, I really like that lamp. I really like that picture. I really like that chair...." Shopping became very frustrating for me. We certainly could not afford all those things—why was she placing all those demands on our family finances? (p. 9)

Later, as Judson and his wife talked about it, he realized that when his family went into a store saying they liked an item, it meant that the item was going to be purchased. Nancy's family, on the other hand, would go into stores just to window-shop. Saying, "I like that," was just expressing an appreciation for the item with no intention to buy.

Some of us learn to assume too much. For example, a husband or wife who refuses to do a task in the house when the other has requested it many times, is communicating non-verbally. The other spouse reacts based on the message he/she *assumes* is being sent.

What message *is* being sent? We have learned from understanding various survival strategies that there are many possibilities. Is it, "I will not be controlled" or "If I fail, I might be criticized, so it is safer not to try," or "Since my needs aren't being met, I am going to punish him in return," or is it another message? We must not assume! Scripture tells us to cast down speculations. They hinder our knowledge of God and our experience of His promises. And we must respond to the other in love *regardless of the motive or meaning.*

Is your old tendency to assume the worst and mind read motives? Following are some hints that may be helpful to you in learning to communicate more effectively with your spouse. You must practice these skills with an attitude of surrender and with the mind of Christ. If that is not the case, they will be practiced selfishly and you can be disappointed. You can utilize these skills even when your spouse does not.

Helpful hints for learning to communicate more effectively

1. **Clarify.** Be specific. Avoid *hinting* or speaking in code for something you would like. Avoid criticizing your mate for not giving it in hopes that the criticism will cause him or her to know what you want! **Ask** for what you desire. Many of those I counsel have said if they have to *ask* for what they want, then it won't mean anything to get it! We must understand that people aren't born with the intuition for knowing what others are thinking. Besides, that is playing games. State directly what your desire is without accusing or demanding. *It is okay to ask for what you want, but this must be done while letting go of presumed "entitlements." As you depend on the Lord, you must be content and satisfied if your spouse does not give it.* If he or she doesn't, say, "I'm sorry you don't feel that way, but I'll be okay."

2. **Be open about your opinions.** This does not mean putting down your spouse. We are talking about communicating with love. Remember, it is okay if you disagree. Your mate disagreeing with you doesn't mean that he or she is disrespecting you or rejecting you. If your spouse gets angry when you have a different opinion, it doesn't mean you shouldn't have respectfully stated your view-

point. So do not be threatened and shut down. Intimacy doesn't require having the same opinions.

3. **Surrender Survival Strategies.** Let go of the ways you continue the power struggle such as defensiveness, attacks and counter-attacks, threats and so on.

4. **Avoid jumping to conclusions.** Scripture says we are not to speculate! Speculation can cause huge problems. Don't assign motives to the other's behavior. Don't assume. Clarify. Do ask "What do you mean?" or "What do you think about such and such?" Avoid asking, "Why," because it can seem accusing and may lead to your partner's defensiveness.

5. **Listen.** *Seek to understand more than to be understood.* Perhaps you will need to repeat to your mate what you heard him say to let him know you heard him and value what he said (even if you have another opinion). This is sacrificial. Often knowing they have been heard *is all someone wants.* Proverb 18:13 says, "He who gives an answer before he hears, it is folly and shame to him." Folks usually do not hear what another is saying because they are so focused on getting their *own* point across. They may not realize they constantly interrupt and talk over others.

6. **Avoid giving solutions.** This is a BIG one. Unless asked for, it is likely that solutions are not wanted or needed. *And do not preach.* Often a marital partner expresses disappointment over a situation and the mate quickly gives advice on how it should have been done or what could be done differently to fix the situation when the partner just wanted to vent and know he was heard and cared about. You are not responsible for fixing your spouse.

7. **Do not disqualify.** Do not disqualify your partner's emotions or opinions—even if they are wrong. Sometimes, people are told they shouldn't feel or think a certain way or that what they think is absurd. This is not love. Proverbs 15:28 says, "The heart of the righteous ponders how to answer...."

8. Limit discussions. When discussing a highly contentious issue, keep it to that one issue. Do not bring up the past. Do not criticize or attack. Be in a state of forgiveness.

More ideas:

- ❑ Say, "I appreciate you for loving me." This honors your mate

- ❑ Remember to show respect, considering your mate to be better than yourself

- ❑ Pray and/or have devotions together for five minutes each day

- ❑ Always remember that true love is sacrificial, a willingness to come out of your comfort-zone and serve

- ❑ Find ways to say, "I love you" that are based on your partner's "love language"

- ❑ Ask, "How can I show love to you?"

- ❑ Forgive quickly

- ❑ If you have sinned against your mate, ask, "Will you forgive me?"

- ❑ Loving always includes humility and a willingness for weaknesses to be exposed

- ❑ Be willing to learn what your mate's sexual partialities are. Be willing to share what you enjoy

- ❑ Eliminate, "you always," "you never," "you should," "you shouldn't" and "I can't" from your vocabulary!

Learning to Love: Tony and Katrina

The next time Tony and Katrina returned to counseling, they were sitting close to each other. Tony had on a blue company shirt. Something was different. He smiled, leaned forward and clasped the palms of his hands together. I knew he was eager to tell me something. He reminded me that the accusations he had made of Katrina having an affair when she came in late and was too tired for sex were born out of feelings of rejection and hurt—typical emotions he had struggled with all of his life.

He then revealed a little of the way he had privately struggled come to a new and deeper resolve to be content in Christ and learn to love and give himself up for Katrina regardless of her actions and his emotions. He said, "I made the decision to choose to set my mind all during the day on truths you have taught us. I thought it would be harder than it was, but I definitely had to discipline myself to do it.

"When Katrina came in late one evening and turned her back to me as she had many times, I found that I could focus on the Lord, which I did. My feelings were at about "8" or "9" out of a "10," but I wanted to experience the Lord's fulfillment in my life. So I just decided to say something encouraging rather than telling her how hurt and angry I was, which I normally would have done. I prayed for the Lord to give me contentment. I reminded myself that Katrina's actions were from her own issues and had nothing to do with my worth as a man. I was surprised and glad to find that after a few minutes, my emotions began to come down and I was peaceful.

"This was so different for me. Sometimes I've tried to get her to change and give me what I need by punishing her! But I've chosen a few times now not to pursue sex until she is rested and ready. "

Katrina added, "I have noticed the change. It is so *good*. It is encouraging to me. Tony has been volunteering to help and he doesn't demand or seem to expect anything in return."

Tony was open when he said, "In the past, I didn't mind helping, but I thought it was unfair if I didn't get my needs met in return. Now, though, I'm choosing to surrender that kind of attitude. It's all different than I thought. But I do believe that my 'kicking for fairness,' as you phrase it, has prevented me from experiencing God's emotional healing."

Katrina said, "I admit I used my fatigue from long hours at work as an excuse to avoid intimacy, and I need to arrange it so I can be with Tony more even if I can't change my hours right now. He has told me this would encourage him and say *love* to him. But I felt that since his accusations were false, I had a right to work those hours. I know that isn't love but self-centeredness on my part. You've told us that God's purpose in marriage is all about us learning to love and sacrifice our ways for each other.

"I've considered all of this, and I'm willing to trust God for my emotions. In fact, I've already made some choices to spend time with Tony. I found that I've had to focus on the Lord's truths even when I didn't feel it. But I'm gradually experiencing peace I've never had before. In the past, I would just ask the Lord to change my circumstances and when He didn't, I thought He couldn't be trusted."

This counselor was being blessed! This kind of session was what we all had worked diligently toward. It wouldn't be long before Tony and Katrina wouldn't be in counseling every week.

You may be wondering, if you surrender old strategies and allow Christ to live His life out through you, how will you know what to do? You will find that He will give you an idea, inspire you with a thought or the right words, and remind you of what you've learned if your focus is continually on listening to that 'still, small voice' of the Spirit and not the louder voice of self.

Learning to love: Darryl and Mattie

Darryl and Mattie each came to see me for a couple of individual sessions. They wanted me to give some specific ideas on how they could show love to the other. I had given them some ideas and was waiting to see what the outcome would be.

Toward the end of one of Darryl's sessions, he was unusually reflective. He simply said, "I am praying that God will love Mattie through me."

This was tremendous. I was joyful to hear this from a man who had been rigid, prideful, stubborn and erudite and who withdrew into his own world much of the time.

A week later, Mattie came for her time with me. Her ankles weren't crossed and she didn't sit quite as straight and proper as before. She promptly announced she had a lot to tell me. I'd never seen her as expressive as when she sat on the edge of my sofa that day.

"I will begin by reminding you of how Darryl has never supported my relationships with my family and friends," she said. "Well, it was a

Wednesday, three days before my annual Christmas party for my friends. The next day, Thursday, was the day Darryl had promised to help get all the decorations up. Since we were very busy that Wednesday, we went out to eat dinner with the kids. In the restaurant, he blew me away when he told me that he had some clients he had to see and just couldn't help me on Thursday but he would on Friday. I really lost it, Anne. This was just one more thing that said he didn't care about me or appreciate me.

"I had been learning to walk with my mind focused on Christ as my sufficiency, choosing to leave Darryl's and others' responses to me in His hands. I hadn't criticized Darryl for quite a while even though it had been hard for me to ignore my emotions and the thoughts I had. Darryl had actually mentioned one night that he had noticed a change and expressed how much he appreciated it.

"But that night I snapped, and I began fearing what my friends would think of me if the house wasn't just perfect. I accused him of not caring for me and the kids. I was raising my voice and crying and I brought up everything from the past. I knew it was wrong but I couldn't seem to stop. I felt as if I were losing my mind. I knew the children and Darryl were humiliated as we sat there in the restaurant. I admit I've done this in the past, and Darryl was defensive and harsh with me. He withdrew for days. But something different happened this time. And I want to tell you I saw Christ, and I saw Him in Darryl."

I was, to say the least, amazed at this, wondering what was next. Mattie went on to say, "Usually Darryl will react harshly and distance from me. But he just listened and acknowledged what I said. We went home and he acted as if nothing happened, which was puzzling.

"The next evening, he actually came home early and got the decorations up much sooner than I expected. When the children were in bed, he came to where I was standing and asked me if he could hold me. Then we sat down and he asked if I would forgive him for not being attentive to me, for not showing love as he should and for withdrawing when things got rough. I could hardly believe it. He expressed his love and caring. *I tell you I have been so convicted by this.* It has had the greatest effect on me. I experienced Darryl loving me with Christ's love."

She continued. "When I asked Darryl why he decided to respond in this way, he said he had chosen at the restaurant to ignore his feelings of humiliation and failure and focus on his identity in Christ and the Lord's faithfulness and not to react out of his hurt. He said he'd been carefully considering how to respond to me based on what you had told him, Anne. He revealed that he had been choosing to focus on the truth every day from early in the morning. I can't *tell* you what this has meant to me."

I silently praised God. This was a huge breakthrough for Mattie and Darryl. They had begun to learn by experience what love and a walk after the Spirit is all about. They would "fall down" as they walked and would need to be reminded to get back up and start over. But they would never be the same again. *They had taken a journey to the cross.*

Chapter 21

Love Has Nothing to Do with It

On the Map: In Egypt

Counterfeiting: Joe's addiction

Joe's vibrant silk shirts had been bold with a Caribbean flavor and they fit easy. The clothing and the swagger in his walk disguised his sensitivity, his fears and his emotional pain.

Joe was into counterfeiting. He was caught in the snare of pornography and sexual addiction. He had been introduced to it as a teenager for fun and excitement. Now it had become his escape from low self-concept, fear of intimacy and fear of responsibility—his place of "safety" and comfort.

With Joe, as with others, the addiction begins as a search to fulfill neediness and that desire without a name. It can become a counterfeit—a substitute—for the intimacy and passion one may fear with a real person.

Chasing sexual fantasy doesn't require intimacy or vulnerability. *The mental pursuit creates a high, a euphoria, which can become addictive.* Brain chemistry gradually changes so that it takes more and more fantasy of increasingly aberrant images to bring emotional and physical arousal and the euphoria one believes will bring satisfaction. Sexual addiction can happen before the person realizes it. *The result is that one can suddenly find that he has taken a dizzying, racing fall into a prison of his own making.* And there is no fulfillment.

He is entangled in an *affair of the mind* in which he suffers guilt after the episode of fantasy and self-stimulation, saying he will never do it again. The guilt, in turn, can finally send him back into the escape, creating a vicious cycle. There are those who believe there is nothing wrong with this *affair of the mind.*

Addiction to pornography becomes the ultimate avoidance as one hides behind the walls of his own prison. No one ever thinks his quest can lead to a cell with a locked door. But when one is behind that door, he deludes himself into thinking that he cannot have a normal emotional or sexual relationship because of his partner's shortcomings. His mind manufactures a myriad of excuses. He blames his wife and she blames herself. Then, suddenly, at some point, there is his despair of realizing that he has lost control and is in a pit from which he cannot deliver himself.

The problem of lust and sexual addition to pornography and/or mental imagery is in *epidemic proportions* within marriages. Freedom can begin to be experienced only when one receives Christ, learns his identity as a new creation, learns of Christ's indwelling life, understands the fact that sin no longer has any power over him and that he has been set free from the law of "thou-shall-not."

Often, a man will be under the impression that when he looks at a woman and has a sexual urge, this is lust. However, this is temptation. This is not lust. Lust is conceived in the mental pursuit of taking the image and fanaticizing about it.

One's renewing his thoughts to truth and choosing to live out of Christ's life within can empower him to journey with God rather than with his *affair of the mind.* It's the same process that we have described for anyone to be released into the Lord's freedom and peace. He must learn to cast down imaginations by instantly taking every thought captive to the obedience of Christ. He must let go of old myths, self-concepts and entitlements to focus on God's sufficiency for him.

The journey out is one of difficult choices to set and discipline his mind, and he will need encouragement from others. Support from others who understand living under grace rather than law and who have a passion for Christ, can be immensely helpful.

Latoya: What about separation?

The wife *feels* as if there is an affair—whether she is aware of the addiction or not. She feels rejected as a wife and a woman. She is quite often left in a reeling tempest of confusion if she *does* find him caught in sexual unfaithfulness with a person or masturbating after refusing to have sex with her. In all of this, he usually blames her. If it isn't one reason, it is another. And love has nothing to do with it.

It was devastating to Latoya who had believed Joe when he said he had gotten involved in porn because she had gained a few pounds. The wife must come to an understanding of her identity in Christ and relinquish her own strategies while focusing on the truth.

When the wife sees that her husband's addiction has nothing to do with *her* but is born out of his own issues, she can begin to accept him and respond to him with the mind of Christ. This also can help in his walking in the freedom from that bondage that Christ has provided for him.

Latoya had wrestled with thoughts of separating from Joe because of her concern that the children would discover the pornography and/or be affected by his involvement. Because he was beginning to be verbally abusive and was forcing a few unusual sexual practices, she had looked for a way out of the marriage. But since she now had the new focus of knowing Christ as her life and surrendering old strategies while responding in love, she was re-considering her thoughts of separation or divorce.

When Latoya asked me what I thought she should do about this, my answer was that I don't tell individuals what they should do regarding separation or divorce. *She needed to ask herself if her pursuit of knowing God in the ways we had discussed could remain the priority of her heart, soul and mind while choosing to leave.*

Sometimes, individuals and couples who come to me for counseling want to know if it is okay, or if it would be a sin, to separate or divorce. *I believe they are asking a question with the wrong focus.* When people ask this question, their intention is usually to find a way out rather than to be consumed with Christ. In other words, *the thinking is on how much one can "get by with" and still be acceptable to God, rather than on being conformed to His image.* When that is the focus, he or she may have an expectation of marrying again sooner or later.

My response to this question usually is, "This is a matter between you and the Lord. You must ask yourself if you can leave the relationship with the desire and focus of your heart being on knowing Christ as your source."

According to both Paul's and Christ's teachings in Mark 10:1–12, two believers should not divorce. When a spouse says that she believes the mate is being adulterous in his heart and having an affair of the mind when he is addicted to pornography, I agree. However, as I understand it, when Scripture speaks of adultery as related to marriage, it is referring to *ongoing physical*, not mental, infidelity.

If one spouse is a believer and the other is not, then the believing partner should stay with the unbeliever. If the unbelieving partner chooses to separate, then the believer must accept it. (The believing one should not have provoked it in any way.) Nothing is said here about a second marriage for the believer. (1 Corinthians 7:10–13; NASB commentary p. 1735).

Latoya's next questions were, "If I choose to stay, should I try to do something about any pornography coming into the home?" and "Does submission include going along with unusual sex?"

My answer to the first question was that I believed she first should let Joe know her intentions to destroy any such materials as videos and magazines and then do it. *There is no value in nagging, criticism or put-downs as she walks after the Spirit.* Destroying the pornography is not to be an endeavor to change Joe.

She could cancel any television sources, repeatedly if necessary. She could cancel any Internet Service Provider (ISP) allowing the pornography to come in, then subscribe to an ISP that filters any such materials at their ISP site. But the best protection for the family at the time of this writing would be a filtering software like MaxProtect™ that filters all 65,000 of the Internet's communication ports—not just two of the ports as other controls. It provides the most comprehensive Internet activity reports, which can be accessed from anywhere in the world. It can be used with *any* high speed Internet service. MaxProtect™ can be used with television and DVDs as well, with multiple settings and choices. *Latoya must not allow this to become a battle-zone in which she struggles, pushes or snoops to remove the pornography from the home.*

Latoya's concern was that if she did destroy materials and instill filtering software, Joe might become physically abusive. In that case, I advised Latoya to report the abuse, leave and go to a safe place with the children, remembering that Joe's behavior is not her fault! She will need encouragement to continue *to respond to Joe with the attitude of Christ* as she takes responsibility for herself and the children. If the violent behavior on Joe's part continued, then I believe separation would be in order.

Often victims of physical abuse believe they deserve to be punished or see themselves as helpless. When they begin to believe their identity in Christ, they can learn to think and respond differently, drawing boundaries and taking responsibility for themselves. They will need support in this new and unfamiliar territory from a Christian counselor or support group.

The answer to Latoya's second question was that she should say, "No," to any sexual practices that have to do with bondage, sadism, bestiality, homosexuality, multiple partners and the like. We addressed the definition of submission in Chapter 19. Agreeing to *anything* one's spouse wants is *neither* submission *nor* a servant's heart. That kind of behavior might even result from a fleshly pattern of dependency or co-dependency, which needs to be surrendered.

I emphasized that Latoya's motive in refusing to have pornography in the house and refusing hurtful sexual practices is not to be a *fleshly* attempt to protect herself emotionally, or to hurt Joe, because her focus must be on Christ in her as her source of protection, fulfillment, adequacy and strength.

First Corinthians 7:3–5 says that each marital partner has the power to sexually fulfill the other and should do so, not withholding themselves from each other unless it is by mutual agreement for a time of prayer. Then they should come back together. In cases where there has been a physical affair and the offended mate chooses to stay in the marriage, they should seek counseling and there should be assurance there is no sexual disease that would be transmitted before usual sexual activity resumes.

And love has nothing to do with it.

Chasing the sexual fantasy doesn't require
intimacy or vulnerability.

The mental pursuit creates a high, a euphoria,
which can become addictive.

As one is caught up in this euphoria of the mental pursuit, brain chemistry gradually changes so that it takes more and more fantasy of increasingly aberrant images to bring emotional and physical arousal and the euphoria one believes will bring satisfaction. Sexual addiction can happen before the person realizes it.

The result is that one can suddenly find
that he has taken a dizzying, racing fall
into a prison of his own making.

Chapter 22

R&R: Recapping and Reflecting

On the Map: In Canaan. Our couples recap their marital journeys.

Tony and Katrina: Recapping

Tony relaxed with his arm on the back of my sofa. He seemed like a teddy bear again. He was still suntanned and swarthy from being outside overseeing the building construction downtown. But his boots had no mud on them; that was strange....

Katrina still wore her slacks well. She still fingered her earring and crossed her long legs. But her foot had ceased jiggling weeks ago. And she no longer stared in her lap. Her face was open and she smiled.

I hadn't seen them for a while, but they were getting close to "going on maintenance," as they wanted to call it. They felt they were at a point where they no longer needed to see me regularly. There were some difficult times as they were learning to trust God and focus on responding to each other with the attitude of Christ. However, knowing difficulties would come, they now had the encouragement to move forward when they *did* happen.

Both were beginning to be aware of that still small voice of the Spirit convicting and reminding them of truth. This enabled them to respond correctly when old emotions returned. As a result, the difficult times were not as intense and there were fewer of them. It was comforting to them to know growth in Christ is a lifetime process.

I asked Tony and Katrina to recap their experience in counseling and tell me what had been most significant. Katrina's reply was typical. She said, "You know, I considered myself a Christian, and I thought I knew what it was to live the Christian life. But most of what I'd believed for so long wasn't true. I had been taught the Christian life was lived by struggling to put away sinful behaviors and trying hard to perform well enough to please God and others. Instead, I'm learning that it takes discipline to believe God's promises and to continually renew my thinking to the truth about myself in Christ.

"I knew I didn't measure up and I identified myself by what I did. *You taught me that I had my "do" and my "who" mixed up!* The message of grace helped me to know that God has *made me accepted and righteous in Christ, and it isn't based on anything I can do.* I realize now my whining, 'I can't ever do anything well enough to please you!' was just self-pity."

Katrina added, "I thought my lack of wholeness was because God had allowed so much loss in my life. I thought I could not get over the abuse. I was bitter, suspicious and I expected to be *victimized* and rejected.

"I had resentment toward a lot of people. I thought they hated me, because I felt I didn't measure up and didn't deserve love. I nursed and rehashed my wounds and the injustices I had experienced. I didn't want others to see my mistakes, so I denied them by telling anyone who questioned something I did or said that he or she 'just misunderstood me.' The Lord has shown me it was really all about *me* and that I am not called to *get* but to surrender old strategies and, in doing so, I will be filled with Him."

She added, "I thought I had a right to my husband making *me* happy, yet I resented it when I felt I had to perform a certain way in order for *him* to feel satisfied!"

I turned to Tony and asked what he had learned. He said, "I never considered myself super-spiritual, even though I was a believer. But I also had many wrong beliefs, myths, as you call them. So, trying to live in my relationships was just too much. My emotions controlled me and I was bitter and worn-out most of the time. All of this was evident with the failed marriages we both had experienced."

He said, "I'd believed as long as I can remember that a man must see to it he has respect from his spouse and his employees to know he is of worth as a man. I've learned that I am not entitled to that. I thought I was entitled to Katrina having a clean house and hot food on the table when I came home. That would have told me I was worthwhile and that she cared about me. When I didn't get these things I was full of resentment and anger. Both of us thought the marriage was a mistake because our own neediness wasn't being satisfied. You helped us to see that all of our needs can be grouped under *Contentment, Security* and *Worth*, and they all must be met by God."

Tony continued, "It blew me away to understand I am actually united with Christ and that God gave me Christ's life to be lived out through me. Just to know I can enjoy His abundant life and I don't have to perform for His acceptance was major. It still blows my mind to think He will live His life through me if I surrender my old ways and renew my mind. Both of us should submit to and serve each other, but I am learning not to look to Katrina's being obedient to God for *me* to be okay.

"I haven't experienced much yet, but I have begun to know some of His peace. Anne, peace was so unfamiliar that when Katrina worked long hours and I didn't see her much for several days, I thought I didn't care anymore when I wasn't upset about it. Being upset if things weren't right used to mean that I cared!"

I turned to Katrina and said, "I recall how revealing it was for you to come to a new understanding of forgiveness and learn the roles of husband and wife. And it was astonishing to you both to see God's purpose in allowing adversity in marriage. I am grateful that you now know the truths that will set you free and bring you into intimacy with God and each other."

Darryl and Mattie: Recapping

We were nearing the end of Mattie and Darryl's five months of counseling. I was summarizing where we had come from when Mattie spoke up. "It has been made clear to me that we live in a world that says love is *getting*: getting *my* way, making *me* feel good. And I tried to get it by having more, being the best in every area, having the greatest personality, manipulating others to appreciate me by my people-pleasing. I was dependent on others in this way. I did this subtly while guarding myself so others couldn't see how inadequate I really felt."

After understanding her new identity in Christ and His grace, Mattie was in the process of surrendering her manipulative, people-pleasing ways in exchange for sacrificial love that demands nothing in return. **In doing so, she was setting some proper boundaries between herself and others.** I had helped her to see that we do not set boundaries for *others* but for *ourselves*. She was beginning to experience her completeness in Christ rather than struggling to find it in "we-ness" between her and Darryl and in her performance. She had learned the difference in true submission and people-pleasing. Mattie was learning that being kind and giving is not based on what she *thinks* others would like.

"I am aware now how 'I love you' really has meant 'I *need* you' to me and most other people. I remember the acronym T.I.R.E.D. you shared with us in the beginning of our counseling. That was exactly how I felt for so many years." Mattie continued, "Something hit me in my Bible study group yesterday. It was pointed out that the definition of a fool is one who is bloated with himself. He is one who has many words to speak. I have been guilty of that. I had been so full of me that I didn't consider Darryl."

Darryl looked at Mattie and said, "Just as one who avoids and isolates himself for protection is full of himself. And I have been guilty of that."

Mattie went on, "I was beating up on myself and thought I wasn't doing something right, because Darryl was always so unhappy, but you helped me to see that I can't judge myself by outcomes in another person or by what someone else thinks. When I saw Darryl respond to me in love, I decided if he could risk doing that, I could trust God for what my Christmas-party ladies thought of me!"

"If you don't mind, I'd like to say something," Darryl interjected. "I've said it before, but I believe I speak for both of us now. What we have learned needs to be taught everywhere. It is so different than we have been trained to think. Neither of us, and especially I, had no clue about what love really is. You have taught us that it is self-sacrifice. It is laying down my way, my comfort, my protections and my demands in deference to another.

"I had been afraid to love and really didn't know how to live it out practically. You illustrated what it would look like in our individual sessions. I was afraid of the criticism and rejection that might come if I humbled myself. But I am learning to walk through my fear, and I am finding strength and peace beyond anything I would have thought.

"When I went over and opened myself to show caring for Mattie in response to her outburst without avoiding, explaining or being defensive, I learned a great lesson. *It felt like death to me—and I guess it was, in a way.* But I guess it was freedom, too. I'd always thought that kind of response on my part would reinforce her outbursts and cause her to manipulate more. I know it had to be the Lord loving through me, because I was never able before to love her by all my trying."

Mattie added, "I had tried all my life to be filled with externals, busyness, involvement with people. I'd always believed the saying, 'If you do all you can, then God will do the rest.' I tried to analyze, figure and plan everything to death, and I wanted God to bless *my* plans so things would go *my* way. I always wound up frustrated and disappointed and critical of Darryl and then rationalized why my plans didn't work. I finally understand that the Lord must do anything that has any substance or that is lasting."

I responded, "You believed that if you delighted yourself in the Lord, he should *bless your plans in order to give you the desires of your heart!* But you found out that in Psalm 37:4, the word *delight* in Hebrew means "to be pliable or soft and moldable," like that clay that the potter has pounded and punched. When our heart is yielded to His shaping and conforming us by our circumstances and we delight in going with *His* way, that is when we receive the desires of our heart and enjoy abundant peace."

Mattie continued, "My pride of life has been worshipping order in hopes it would bring contentment and peace. I also protected what little worth I could muster by refusing to make decisions. I would control Darryl and others to make them for me. One way I did this was by asking if they 'wanted me to do so and so.' Their "yes" or "no" would place the responsibility and blame on *them* so I would never have to look bad and risk rejection.

"Anne, your observation that I seemed to need to know everything about everybody was right. You helped me become aware of always anxiously glancing to see what others' expressions and reactions were to conversations, and I found that Scripture says we aren't to do that! You pointed out that others noticed me doing it. I used both of these strategies so that I could adjust myself to others to avoid rejection. Now that I am aware of my strategies and why I've held to them, I can set my mind on God's faithfulness to meet my needs."

In conclusion, Darryl said, "I want to tell you of a couple more things I have learned. Deference or submission isn't saying you can't do any better, and humility isn't thinking poorly of myself. When I choose to humble myself and let go of my defenses of avoidance, rationalizing and blame, I may risk looking 'less than' to others, but I decided that God is responsible for justifying me, and now I want to leave what others think of me up to Him."

Latoya: Recapping

I was surprised to see Latoya's hair down. It was *long*. She looked so different that I must have stared. She said, "I see you're noticing I've changed my appearance a little. I'm feeling so free that I bought some casual clothes and I decided on a new hairstyle." She had arrived at her last session with me.

When I asked Latoya if she would summarize her experience in counseling, she said, "I have become aware of so much about myself, my beliefs and expectations and how they were formed. *I have seen how an individual's patterns will be perpetuated through the generations unless he makes hard choices to stop them by living in truth and **having intimate fellowship with God**.* I didn't know that it was really possible to live victoriously. I have found that it *is* possible if I am willing to pay the price, or 'toll,' as you call it, to journey on a new highway. And that price is *my giving up on my fleshly strategies to trust God in all areas!*"

I said, "You have stood firm as your family disapproved of your new walk of faith. It is so opposite to what you learned in the world—to relinquish control, pride and defensiveness rather than to hold on to those things."

"I was taught that the only way out of the darkness of poverty and oppression was to assert myself in the strong, independent fleshly ways I

262

developed. And that's not saying there is anything wrong with perseverance, as long as it is based on my depending on the Lord. It hasn't been an easy choice to focus on my union with Christ and my righteousness in Him as my worth and security and let go of my anger and criticism toward Joe for not being responsible and for the pornography. Instead of pushing to make him be more responsible, and making excuses for him, I am beginning to allow him to experience the natural consequences of his actions."

I volunteered, "You are learning the difference between having a servant's attitude and rescuing Joe from irresponsibility. You told me how you were responding in love to Joe in your daily interactions while setting your mind on Christ. You also found that Joe doesn't withdraw as much since you quit your accusations and your pursuit to get him involved. He is more available."

"Yes, he's noticed and even complimented the change in me, which was very surprising," Latoya replied. "But at first, when I told Joe of my intention to not rescue him and to not waver in disposing of whatever pornography I knew about, at first he went into a rage and withdrew. When I remained constant in my decision to back off, he even started pursuing me some, telling me how sorry he was for not being involved with the family and so on. Then he tried to sweet-talk me into covering up something wrong he did.

"When Joe realized that I did not intend to go back to my old ways, even though I have more of a servant's heart and am more supportive and respectful of him, to my shock *his rage grew worse*. But I made some hard choices to fix my focus on God's provision and not revert to my old rescuing and pursuing Joe to change. He has begun to turn around and be a little more involved. Not that he doesn't show his anger at times, but he doesn't have as much to fight against now!"

She slid forward to sit on the edge of my sofa and smiled, "I am starting to believe that 'love never fails.' Being kind and gentle to Joe in the face of what he has done could only happen by Christ in me. I was quite confused at first when you explained that God has a purpose for the adversity in our lives and in marriage. But if it hadn't been for the unfairness, I wouldn't have come to surrender. I wouldn't have learned what real love is."

Latoya said, "The things I have been taught here are so opposite to what we learn in society and in some churches I've been in. I'm not consistent in this walk, but I'll never be the same again. I have already been filled with the Lord's peace and personal assurance beyond my comprehension. The anger and depression have gone. I am so grateful," she said.

Latoya's choosing loyalty to Joe over her family and friends was involved in her transformation. She revealed, "Since that is hard for my family to understand, I've had to focus my thoughts constantly. The grace support group you recommended has been tremendously helpful with this. Joe has not changed much, but the outcome in *me* has been amazing. I believe I am beginning to know the Lord."

Anne: My reflections

October leaves rustled on our hill. Two eagles soared, dipped and lifted high as sunset closed a crisp, blue day. I thanked God for filling my longing to be lifted as if on eagles' wings and for teaching me that Jesus Christ is the name of my desire to soar high and free...my desire that once had no name.

"Yet those who wait for the LORD Will gain new strength; They will mount up with wings like eagles, They will run and not get tired, They will walk and not become weary" (Isaiah 40:31).

After He delivered them from their captivity in Egypt, God said to Israel, *"I bore you on eagles' wings and brought you to Myself."* His expanding breath of life has nurtured and satisfied both Vinson and me within our marriage. He has filled our emptiness and driven away our loneliness. He has strengthened, protected and blessed far beyond all we could ever ask or think. But learning to love and patiently wait on Him is an ongoing process.

The eagles reminded me of the day years ago when I sat on the steps of the old country church. I recalled the pastor's words, "Brothers and sisters, we have come together tonight to observe communion and the washing of the saints' feet, because Jesus Christ said, 'Do this in remembrance of me.' After partaking of the bread and wine, the ladies will gather on the front pews on right side of the church and the men on the left. You will take a pan of water and a towel and proceed with our observance of washing the saints' feet. In doing this we signify Christ's love by our willingness to humble ourselves before one another and serve one another."

I reflected on how all but one of the travelers with whom we became acquainted have arrived in a new homeland where they are learning what it means to let humility and a servant's attitude be lived out with their mates. As a result, they are beginning to taste of God's life: His rest, freedom, joy and power.

This does not mean the couples will have no more foes to face. It doesn't mean they won't come to another place of personal brokenness. They will. Trials will come at various times during one's life. But in learning how to respond correctly, they can grow to maturity in Christ, finding personal victory and peace as they live within their most intimate relationships.

Today, I pressed the button on the radio in the car and heard a song tell me that being "caught in a steady rush" is the way love is supposed to be. *Really.* The songs are still offering those beguiling anticipations that promise the right person will bring us the excitement, happiness and completeness we long for and our neediness will be satisfied. When I contrast these illusions with the journey God designed to bring us to His fulfillment, I am amazed.

Recapping the Journey

In this book, the marital journey began with a map. The map depicted God's course or path for believers. It took us from Egypt, where we were imprisoned by our sinful nature and programmed by the world system, across the Red Sea, which represents our new birth.

From there we entered into the wilderness, which is a place of thirst, confusion and defeat caused by living from myths and sinful survival strategies. Leaving the wilderness, God's course and plan carried us across the River Jordan, which depicts death to the old ways. We then entered Canaan, the Promised Land of our inheritance and our travels led to a new highway, a toll road where the abundant life is experienced within our marital relationships.

We became acquainted with some couples as they were needy, lost and struggling in the wilderness. We followed their spiritual progress as they became aware of their old strategies and as they learned of their identity in Christ. We saw their responses as they were taught about the purpose of adversity in marriage. Next, we observed them as they came to surrender and crossed Jordan. We learned how they began allowing the mind of Christ to be worked in them as they traveled with their mates on the toll road in the new territory of Canaan.

Finally, we rejoiced with them as they began to know God's relief and rest as they lived in relation to each other. They began to experience God's filling and completing them and driving away their fear and loneliness—His meeting those most basic needs of *Contentment, Security* and *Worth*. They had searched for life and meaning in each other, but in trusting God and losing dependency on their own strategies, they found the life they had desired.

Lee LeFebre said,

Marriage is truly God's great processing tool, the refiner's fire. Marriage rends us naked, not only in terms of our behaviors, but also in terms of our motivations, attitudes and emotions. It radically reveals the insufficiency of the flesh.

We had no idea in the beginning that our partner's imperfections and our difficulties in marriage would be God's opportunity to bring us into His best, His fulfillment, and for us to glorify Him by being conformed to His image.

Promises in the Promised Land

When we choose to trust the Lord and walk in these paths of Christ's righteousness, the good things with which He satisfies us, the promises we experience, are wonderful, exceeding our ability to comprehend or explain. It is "in the land of the living" that we can walk fulfilled in Him. Many of these precious promises are in prophetic form in Isaiah, 30, 40, 43, 54-58, Jeremiah 29, John 15, Psalm 27 and Psalm 56. I have put them in my own words.

266

- You will have perfect peace.

- Your light shall break forth as the morning and will be bright as noontime.

- Your gloominess will be turned into brightness like midday.

- He will satisfy your hungry soul.

- He will exchange your blanket of heaviness (depression) for a garment of praise.

- Your righteousness in Christ will go in front of you, leading you, and His glory will guard you from the rear.

- You shall be like a tree planted by rivers of living water, and you will bring forth fruit in your season.

- Your recovery will spring forth hastily.

- If you thirst, He will satisfy you with living water so that you will not thirst again.

- He will cause you to ride on the heights of the earth and feed you from your inheritance.

- You will ask what you will, and it shall be done (If you ask and do not receive, it is because you have asked wrongly, in order to consume it on your own desires).

- He will bind up (heal) your broken heart and give release to you where you are imprisoned.

- He will replace your shame of your youth with double honor.

- He will restore the years the locusts have eaten.

- You will walk on a highway where no lion or ravenous beast will harm you.

- If you have been forsaken and storm-tossed and not comforted, he will restore you and comfort you, and in righteousness you will be established.

- Your children will be taught of the Lord, and their well-being will be great.

- He will have great compassion on you, the youthful wife, who was rejected.

- You will be far from oppression. You will not fear. Terror will not come near you, and whoever assails you, God will cause them to fall.

- He will satisfy your mouth with good things.

- You will have unspeakable joy and a peace that exceeds your comprehension.

- Those who devise evil against you shall be trapped in their own snare, and if they dig a pit for you, they will fall in it.

- Since the Lord is your light, strength and salvation, you have no need to fear anyone.

- Others may twist your words, but in the time of trouble, the Lord will hide you in His pavilion, in the cleft of the rock and under his wings.

- You who trust God will remain safe in your soul.

- God has plans for you for good and not evil, plans for you to prosper.

- You will have confidence and assurance forever.

- You will gain new strength and *mount up with wings like eagles*. You will run and not get tired and walk and not become weary.

Bibliography

Allender, Dan and Longman, Tremper P. *Intimate Allies*. Wheaton: Tyndale, 1995.

Anderson & Mylander. *The Christ-Centred Marriage*. Ventura: Regal Books, 1996.

Bell, Steve and Valerie. *Made to be Loved*. Chicago: Moody Press, 1999.

Boone, Wellington. *Your Wife is Not Your Momma*. New York: Doubleday, 1999.

Carnes, Patrick. *Out of the Shadows*. Center City: Hazeldon Educational Materials, 1992.

Chambers, Oswald, *Still Higher for His Highest*. Grand Rapids: Zondervan, 1970.

Chapman, Gary. *The Five Love Languages*. Chicago: Northfield, 1992.

Crabb, Lawrence. *The Marriage Builder*. Grand Rapids: Zondervan, 1982.

Curtis, Brent and John Eldridge. *The Sacred Romance*. Nashville: Thomas Nelson, 1997.

Eagar, Rob. *The Power of Passion*. Suwanee, Ga.: Grace Press, 2002.

Gillham, Bill and Annabel Gillham. *He Said, She Said*. Eugene: Harvest House, 1995.

Groom, Nancy. *Married Without Masks*. Colorado Springs: Navpress, 1989.

Hession, Roy. *The Calvary Road*. Fort Washington: Christian Literature Crusade, 1950, 1990.

The Holman Bible Dictionary. Nashville: Broadman and Holman Publishers, 1991.

LeFebre, Lee. "The False Choice." *The Exchanged life Newsletter, ELM*, 2002.

Mason, Mike. *The Mystery of Marriage*. Portland: Multnomah Press, 1985.

McVey, Steve. *Grace Rules*. Eugene: Harvest House, 1998.

McVey, Steve. *Grace Walk*. Eugene: Harvest House, 1995.

Murray, Andrew. *Abide in Christ*. Fort Washington: Christian Literature Crusade, 1997.

Nee, Watchman. *The Release of the Spirit*. Indianapolis: The Sure Foundation, 1965.

Noonan, Peggy. *When Character Was King*. New York: Viking, 2001.

Rentzel, Lori. *Emotional Dependency*. Downers Grove: Intervarsity Press, 1990.

Silvious, Jan. *Moving Beyond the Myths*. Chicago: Moody Press, 2001.

Stanford, Miles. *Principles of Spiritual Growth*. Lincoln: Back to the Bible, 1987.

Stanley, Charles. *The Blessings of Brokenness*. Grand Rapids: Zondervan, 1997.

Stanley, Charles. *The Source of My Strength*. Nashville: Thomas Nelson, 1994.

Stone, Dan and Greg Smith. *The Rest of the Gospel*. Dallas: One Press, 2000.

Swihart, Judson. *Communication in Marriage*. Downers Grove: Intervarsity Press, 1981.

Tozier, A.W. *The Old Cross and the New*. Brochure.

Trippe, Anne. *The Purpose of Trials and Adversity*. Atlanta: 1993.

Van Vonderan, Jeff. *Families Where Grace is in Place*. Minneapolis: Bethany House, 1992.

The Old Country Church

CSW

* Christ lives this life in me as I surrender my old ways + renew my mind

p259

God meets my basic needs:
- contentment
- security
- worth

* humility + forgiveness = attitude of Christ + letting go of presumed rights + giving up the pursuit of anything other than Christ to bring contentment

Jesus came to heal my soul +
emotions + deliver me from the
hurt of being cheated on, by His
life + truth. It is up to me
to receive the reality of this
p 210

My automatic guardedness +
lack of trust are tied to
my fear of being hurt again.

When I walk after the Spirit, not
demanding my presumed rights, I
am in a state of forgiveness to
others!
p 212

The very power of the cross + the
attitude of Christ is contained in
the act of forgiveness.
p 213

When I forgive others they may not
change but their actions will have
no power over me
p 218

Submission is letting go of my rights,
fleshly protections + preferences   p 228

I love Glenn because I know that God will
protect me + meet my needs.

CPSIA information can be obtained at www.ICGtesting.com
Printed in the USA
LVOW08s1413110414

381352LV00001B/77/P